BEHIND THE SMILE

Acclaim for Book & Author

Stan Frith's poetry anthology will appeal to a wide range of audiences. His beautifully crafted pieces reflect a prodigious range of thoughts, impressions and feelings - love, hate, hope, shame and more. Despite this variation in themes, his poems were written with one goal in mind: to chronicle his understanding of the nature of life. This is the second book of poetry from this naturally gifted author (the very successful *Time in Between* being the first). Both books benefit charities so while his words tells us he is human, his generosity humanitarian. *Lidia Vianu: Writer; Critic; Professor of English at Bucharest University; Consulting Editor "The International Literary Quarterly"; Hon. Editor "Contemporary Literary Horizon" - The London Poetry Society biennial prize for poetry translation.*

Lyrical, tender and profoundly moving, these poems reference the healing heart; broken but bravely optimistic. It is how those of us with depression live; adrift in the dark depths but forever struggling to the sunlit shallows. Here is joy and sorrow but, above all, hope; a gift to life. *Sally Brampton: Writer, journalist and novelist (Three novels and one non-fiction "Shoot The Damn Dog – a memoir of depression). Until recently, eight years Sunday Times "Agony Aunt.*

Sports men and women are not exempt from the pernicious influence of depression. I think I am the only Premier League rugby player to have documented the condition, but the hidden cases of depression in sport are both significant and widespread. I am well aware of the work Depression Alliance is doing to help people and I applaud their work. I also know Stan Frith very well (he lives in Bath and supports Bath Rugby). His reputation, both as an author and for helping others, is legendary. It therefore comes as no surprise he is donating all proceeds from this book to charity. I really hope it does well thereby enabling the charity to do more good work. *Duncan Bell: Retired Bath Rugby and England International rugby player.*

As a songwriter my aim is to write songs that get people thinking. Stan's poetry is not only thought provoking but also conveys messages of joy, love, hope and sorrow. In donating all proceeds to aiding charities that counter depression & addiction, I really congratulate him on his dedicated work. *'Suggs' McPherson: lead singer with the band "Madness", musician and songwriter.*

Stan Frith's poems elegantly and honestly do what poetry does best: try to make sense of their world. *Bel Mooney: Author, journalist and broadcaster.*

Touching and authentic, a cry from the heart' *Tim Lott: Author (five novels and a memoir), journalist, critic, TV/Radio commentator.*

A testament to the power of poetry is its ability to heal self. Though it obviously springs from such palpable sorrow, Frith's writing flows simply and clearly, totally immersing you in its rejuvenating waters. *Rachel Kelly: author of "Black Rainbow - How Words Healed Me: My Journey Through Depression".*

Given the withering impact that depression can have on a mind, not just of those that suffer, but as in the author's case losing a loved one, it is a source of endless fascination to me how well people touched by mental illness write. From William Styron to Andrew Solomon, and from Gwyneth Lewis to Sally Brampton, the canon is rich, moving and learned. Stan Frith's poetry is a touching, elegiac addition to the list. *Mark Rice-Oxley. Guardian International News Editor; author of "Underneath the Lemon Tree – a memoir of depression and recovery"*

Stan Frith's poetry can be uplifting or heart-breaking and all emotions in between. Always an ambitious poet whatever his topic or genre, his desire to apply his talent toward helping others gives us a clue as to what lies behind his smile. *Ian & Paula – Lord & Lady Maclaurin.*

Stan Frith is a man generous with his time and talents and his latest poetry volume is fresh evidence of this. There is plenty of evocative verse here – and plenty to think about. *Lynne Fernquest: Editor, The Bath Chronicle, Somerset Guardian and associated websites.*

His extraordinarily introspective work and the kindness he has shown in wanting to help others can only be described as the epitome of creative altruism. *Douglas Westcott, Author of "Go Swift and Far".*

Behind the Smile by Stan Frith gathers all the secrets, fears, and wonderings about everyday life and makes them into extra-ordinary but accessible poems. This excellent collection of his work can be read, enjoyed and learned from time and time again. *Dave Robinson, Film & Record Producer. Founder of Stiff Records.*

On the road of life, it's not where you go,
but who's by your side that makes a difference.
- Anon

One of the ceaseless wonders of the world:
the power of a smile.
- Malcolm Forbes

Blessed is the influence of one true
loving human soul on another.
- George Eliot

Behind the smiling face lies a
frowning visitation of providence.
- Stan Frith

ACKNOWLEDGEMENTS

As was the case with my first book of poetry
'TIME IN BETWEEN'
all profits from the sale of this book will go to charity.
I have chosen **Depression Alliance** for reasons explained later.
This would not have been possible without generous support from the
following companies or individuals

WITHY KING SOLICITORS
HELPHIRE GROUP plc
FIDELIUS LIMITED
and
Andrew Brownsword Foundation
Deeley Freed Estates Ltd
Barbers Farmhouse Cheesemakers

Also
CPI ANTONY ROWE LIMITED
For producing the book at cost

Also
LOUI JOVER (ARTIST)
http://louijover.tumblr.com
For allowing me to reproduce some of his paintings

Also
PETER SHERRARD (PHOTOGRAPHER)
http://www.petesherrardphotography.com
For the cover photo

.....and of course, the encouragement and support
of my dear wife Angie.

Also by Stan Frith

"The Expatriate Dilemma"
(An international management textbook)
Nelson-Hall ISBN 0 882297015

"A Step In The Right   Direction"
(A political crime novel)
New Horizon ISBN 0 86116914

"Bay at the Moon"
Screenplay - Drama for Television

"Time in Between"
(Book of 100 poems & verse)
Palladian ISBN 978-0-9929591-1-1

Behind The Smile

A collection of over 150 poems and verse
Written
By

Stan Frith

Palladian Books, Bath

BRITISH LIBRARY CATALOGUING IN PUBLICATION DATA
Behind The Smile
1. Frith, Stan 2014
ISBN 978-0-9929591-0-4

Published by Palladian Books, Bath

First printed 2014

Printed in Great Britain
by CPI Anthony Rowe Ltd,
Chippenham,
Wilts SN14 6LH

DEDICATION

Dedicated to the memory of my son Jason who died in 2008.
He was loved dearly and is missed greatly.

Also to each one of you who, in buying this book, perhaps did not
necessarily do so out of a passion for poetry, but in support of this
charitable endeavour.

Many thanks

TABLE OF CONTENTS

FOREWORD

If you have read *Time in Between*, you will already know enough about me not to want to suffer the tedium of reading about me all over again. However, since there might just be one or two of you who did not rush out and grab a copy of *Time in Between* - even though all proceeds went to charity; here I hope, is a palatable synopsis:

A humble beginning (I lived in a council house until my early teens), grafted my way through grammar school, college and university. Acquired a MBA (Masters Degree in Business). Hard work, tenacity and fair share of good fortune resulted in a successful business career and a place on the Boards of several prestigious companies. Always lurking below the surface - a constant desire to write. When time permitted, that is what I did.

A brief introductions to my three other books and screenplay are also covered in the Foreword to '*Time in Between*', as well as on my website *www.stanfrith.co.uk* so if you are not aware of them but are interested, you should get a copy of *Time in Between* or go to my website

This book, **Behind the Smile** is a further 'bringing together' of over one hundred and fifty poems and verse that I have written over the last decade. Some were written to my loving wife Angie, or with her in mind. Initially she was opposed to me publishing them as she considers them private and very personal. However, she finally agreed to me including a number of them after much cajoling and as it is in aid of such a worthy cause.

A lot of these poems were written in 2008, at a time of tremendous sadness and grieving for me. It was when my eldest son Jason died suddenly at age 32, having fought (and lost) a prolonged battle with depression. Looking back at those poems now, I think they most certainly illustrate the heartache, pain and anguish I felt at the time and for which writing was to a degree my catharsis. I share them with you, not to attract sympathy or share misery, but in the hope if ever you have to endure similar sadness, these words may give you comfort.

Many people have an intuitive sense that voice in general and poetry in particular can be healing.

This proved to be the case when I shared with those I love and with friends, the poems I wrote after the loss of Jason. They became a collective path to healing.

It will also give you some insight as to why I chose **Depression Alliance** as my charity of choice, and why I have also become a member of their Appeal Board. All profits from the sale of this book will go to this charity in memory of Jason.

Writing poetry however, is not just a way of coping – that is an over simplification, it is a way of capturing feelings, moments in time – and of remembering. Also of helping others to tap into their emotional self in the hope they will also look beyond today and into the future positively and with optimism.

As a poet there is in my opinion no greater compliment than someone wanting to share in the emotions that you feel, whether they be highs or lows and especially if depression has touched their life and they are working towards healing and growth. If it makes them feel less alone then it is reward enough for any poet.

To ensure that I can once again donate all profits from this book to my chosen charity, I have worked with local companies to get it to market as cost-effectively as possible, eliminating the expense of middlemen. Some might interpret this as an exercise in self-indulgence. However, since the poems are all inspired by the many feelings and experiences gained from my journey through life and touch upon the things I saw and opinions formed along the way, I suppose I could excuse such a critique.

John Whitworth wrote that poems are a part of the memory of the human race, but to become part of memory a poem has to be memorable. Whether any of those contained in this book meet that criterion is for you to decide. However, if *Behind the Smile* generates a significant sum of money for the designated charity (as did *Time in Between)*, then it will have been very worthwhile; if any part of it gives you just a modicum of pleasure, then that will be a bonus.

Stan Frith

BYGONE TOMORROWS

Pause – and understand the wave of sorrows
flowing through life's many rivers,
listen to the sound of sad teardrops,
release the rain of sadness.
Sweeping with love's many heartaches,
feel the tide of wanting a true love,
the ocean is full and wide;
treasures everywhere,
lakes and seas will join together as one.

Think – and motivate the search for tomorrows
streaming through life's different waters,
listen to the sound of new heartbeats,
visualise the cries of laughter.
Smiling with love's different bondings,
feel the joy of living a romance;
the world is full and wide,
treasures everywhere,
hope and faith will join together as one.

Act – and accept love in its truest form
pure since time's first beginning,
renew daily those childhood promises,
unbroken until time's death.
Life is full of bygone tomorrows,
worry not that it does not fulfil all;
let the tide carry you to the horizon of hope
with many memories to savour,
floating serenely to journey's end.

AN ELUSIVE VISION

Who can show me the snowdrop's hidden dwelling
or re-create mystical music from a wind chime?
Behold, inward eyes that promise new beginnings
see visions omnipresent twixt waking and dreaming.

In darkness outside exists an enigma of stark solitude
casting shadows over expanses of barren fields.
Majestic waving willows in moonlight are dancing
to an audience of subdued stars in the sky above.

As the wind chime mournfully plays its mystical refrain,
leaves like feathers from the heavens come falling.
A lifeless earth's picture is captured and framed
and billowing clouds like white smoke are sailing.

The night-time engulfs a tired heart that remembers
a painful moment that has remained forever.
How could a tired heart grasp a moment so frail
and parody a drama of such melancholy?

Unfulfilled promises of stars in candent embers
and a crescent moon that eclipses and obscures.
Eerie mist and torrential rain dampen all around
like Angel's tears falling down on a lonely grave.

Sodden grasses cushion the gasping snowdrops
and the wind-chime music hauntingly lingers.
Like tear drops casting ripples on the lake
waves of anxiety caress darkened shores.

The shadow of shade recedes, the sky is dawning
and a breaking ray of hope brightens the horizon.
A stream of light warms the grasses and snowdrops
and the echo of wind chimes again gently resonates.

Somewhere beyond where the human soul exists
discover that elusive vision twixt waking and dreaming.
Picture the snowdrop's secret, hidden dwelling
and re-create that mystical wind-chime music.

WINGS THAT WHISPER

We all can dream, have fluttering wishes,
those flights of fancy that loneliness brings.
As I drift off to sleep cocooned in my bed,
I see an aerial dancer with golden wings.

Wrapped in a rainbow of vibrant beauty,
instant attraction like butterfly to flower.
Tempted by nature's forbidden fruits,
flattered, enchanted by a seductive power.

Timeless beauty wrapped in a silk cocoon,
teasing with me with a butterfly's kiss.
Cajoling me into chasing rainbows,
carrying me to heights of evanescent bliss.

Yes, yes flaunt your gossamer wings,
fly me to that place called rainbow sky.
Transcend through fabled time and tide,
yet be patient with me, my butterfly.

Enchant the depths of my virgin eyes,
tease me with your the sensual butterfly kiss.
A promise of perfumed dreams,
savouring the moment of rainbow bliss.

A warm glow stirs the embers of my heart,
caressing each other our wings expand.
Drinking in naked, erotic fantasies,
two hearts, two souls collide and land.

Bringing to me a smile on beating wings,
on wings that whisper of secret wishes.
To fly sky high on gossamer wings,
floating on an aroma of lilac kisses.

Dancing to internal rhythms pulsing beat
intoxicated we reach that rainbow sky.
Mind racing, a fluorescent flutter,
don't stop, stay with me, darling butterfly.

Like a romantic melody that greets a new dawn,
tenderly, lovingly my heart sings.
Golden hues of a breaking day wash over me,
as I lay languid beneath emollient wings.

DELICATE PAINTED LADIES (arrest my attention)

On a clear, bright, sunny day, I catch a glimpse
of what is today a rare and beautiful sight.
A multitude of mottled, multicoloured butterflies
fluttering wings and gossamer fragility
tantalisingly etched in bright colours.
A kaleidoscope of artful design
to inspire and aspire.
The endangered Red Admiral making a brave return,
a Swallowtail once feared to be lost to time,
both gems to the butterfly world.
They glide and dance a delicate ballet
among the glorious, luxuriant blooms.
Splashes of radiant splendour,
a metamorphic oasis
against a drab backcloth of urban grey.

Free to swoop and flutter where the wind goes,
riding carefree upon atmospheric tides
or dancing to the virtuosic wind.
Flying high above lush green trees
in clear unblemished skies.
Then floating like autumn falling leaves
gliding fervently on a sun-kissed breeze.
Delicate Painted Ladies, Peacocks and Tortoise Shells
ephemeral beauties arrest my attention.
I am intoxicated by beauty redefined.
They lighten my heart and make me smile
bringing pleasure to my eye.
A symbol of freedom and eternity
filling my dreams
with all the treasures of summer.

INNER STRENGTH

The fountain of my strength and of my resolve
Every aspect of my being, my aspirations
That from which I draw each ounce of energy.

That impetus which constantly drives me onwards
Those triumphant images that decorate dreams
The potent salves that energise and motivate.

Each of the sun's rays that form the morning dawn
That brighten and illuminate every new experience
An epiphany that is real and not just in the mind.

Accolades and congratulations in abundance
Champagne wasted but cooling and anointing
A temporary veiled nobility of the victorious.

The furtive knowledge of self-imposed challenge
Knowing you excelled and achieved greatness
Rest now on laurels of delicately dusted solitude.

Beacons of light on the sable sky of midnight
The ardent blushing of congratulatory handshakes
The resonant 'thank you' of the contented soul.

A POET'S THOUGHTS

I translate thoughts, experiences and emotions
like a mind artist with spectral canvas.
A linguistic painter, lexicologist, phrase-maker.
It is spiritual release, exorcism,
a portrayal of what my eyes see and my heart feels.
When I see spring flowers in bloom
I think of them in terms of poetry.
My words hopefully painting
a colourful, vivid tapestry,
such that even on the greyest of days
they brighten someone's world,
shedding light on their emotions,
lifting spirits, and comforting the soul.

Poets are kindred spirits in their love of nature,
the gift of children and the wonders they bring.
Plants and animals, how they nourish us,
inspire us to want to share through poetry
the beauty of this planet.
When I write of swollen rivers and waterfalls
I hope you feel the cool mist on your face.
When I write of trees in woods and forests
I want you to imagine their noble trunks and limbs
and how closely they resemble people.
When I write about the wild and wayward wind
an awesome chill ought to cloak your body
and send a shiver down your spine.

A WINTER DREAM

Winter has buried our world in alabaster white;
familiar landmarks wear a cloak of new disguise.
Powdery snow gloves the stark fingers of forests
protecting barren, leafless bark with its expectation
of propagation; of reawakening dormant buds.

A meeting point between pristine innocence, gestation
and the veiled, pregnant promise of spring ripening.

Each trunk and limb mirroring the action of man;
stretching to the sky - reaching, arching, swaying.
Creating symmetrical aisles of church-like splendour,
a near holy ordinance, a sacrament to Mother Nature.

Into this temple of nature the innocent may walk
hand in hand toward communion with their Maker.
Inward, toward the birth of their unbridled faith
and outward, toward the celestial, brightening sky.

Terrestrial planets barely visible, like thorny lights
scattered wildly in the blackness of a winter sky.
Pristine stars lovingly polished by Mother Nature
honed until their glistening points are thistle sharp.

With first light, cotton mists rise on shimmering rays
and skyward, birds swoop and dive across the land.
Their unbridled dances wafting, diffusing the mist,
for a moment bringing credence to a Winter dream.

BEHOLD WINTER

Autumn mourning; shedding leaves of amber gold
in death throws, silently falling from skeletal trees.
Likewise, the hawthorn shakes her cloak of ruby fire,
naked, taunting, rhythmically swaying in the breeze.

Winter's chilling breath now lingers eerily in the air,
creating strands of whispered frost, like silver lace.
Deep within the forest a haunting and distant voice
coaxes the snowdrops to dance with chilling grace.

Hark as Winter's orchestra plays keenly on the wind,
and snowflakes dance to her dismal, haunting tune.
Like a manic furrier she drapes the scene in white,
all brides of nature shrouded and steeped in gloom.

Winter's touch transforms spiders' webs to gems,
like diamond necklaces of cold, reflected glass.
Lakes and ponds turn to stone with breathless ease,
frozen daggers forming from each blade of grass.

Winter's kiss enchants the wood into slumbers deep
while the holly spears and stains, her berries bright.
Mistletoe, like a crow's nest, resting on the bough,
berries like strands of pearls reflect a ghostly light.

This Winter symphony plays on throughout the night,
comforting nature as she slumbers in the earth.
In Spring she will re-awaken with the sun's return
thawing the ground and heralding new birth.

THE MIRACLE OF FRIENDSHIP

There's a miracle called friendship
that dwells within our hearts;
we don't know how it happens
or even when it starts.
But the happiness it brings us
definitely gives one a lift,
when you realise that friendship
is life's most precious gift.

There is nothing quite as warming
as someone who always shares;
your laughter and your secrets,
your wishes and your cares.
Someone who will be there
through your good times and tears,
who stays close by your side
as your friend through the years.

Good friends are who we turn to
when our spirits need a lift;
friendships are highly valued
more than any other gift.
True friends fill each of our lives
with beauty, joy, and grace,
making life much more bearable
and the world a happier place.

WOVEN WORDS

My poems are words woven,
like a tapestry of gold
and silver thread.
Occasionally reflecting sunlight
or a bright, starry night.
Is that what you read?

Were you left breathless,
stunned by naked truth,
no sun or stars overhead?
A tapestry that is threadbare
dull, like angry clouds.
Is that what you read?

MY REFLECTION

Light playing over wintry, frosted glass,
blacked-out windows watching them pass.
Dark eyes searching for imperfection.
What do I see in my reflection?

Stars in the water, foretellers of fate,
shimmering eerily while I patiently wait.
Wishing for just a modicum of affection.
What do I see in my reflection?

Cracked mirror hanging against the wall,
window of a soul, shows nothing at all
An echo of a sigh makes no connection.
Sadness I see in my reflection.

WINTER THROUGH THE EYES OF ARTIST & ACTOR

It is autumn.........

A breath of chill wind raises my vigilant senses
and colourful leaves dance around me.
The sun's ebbing rays, reflecting from the lake
fleetingly nestle me in warmth.
But out of sight, winter eagerly lies in wait
in the wings of this autumn theatre.
One chilled, frail debutant flower
anticipating the coming of winter
trembles in the autumn breeze
like an opening night thespian.
Beneath the denuded, timorous trees
autumnal litter abounds.
Today's colourful, kaleidoscope trails
and bright painted horizons
must soon make way
for the artist's winter palette.

In acknowledging the arrival of winter winds,
row upon row of well-mannered trees
like stately Japanese businessmen
bow augustly and in unison.
Night creature choirs sing a chorus
while the soloist owl too-woos.
Through the naked ghost-like branches
white candescent snowberries
illuminate the winter gloom.
An interval; nature's audience is resting,
flowers drift off into gentle sleep.
The final act is about to take centre stage
and a shimmering, wintry dawn sun,
like a candle-powered spotlight,
paints a backcloth of snow-topped peaks,
mirrored in crystal clear water.

There exists a unique stillness on cold winter nights
that is broken only by the crack of ice-laden boughs.
Icy abstractions and crystalline concoctions
form part of the artist's winter inspiration.
Frost-coated limbs of slope-shouldered trees
droop drowsily down as if asleep,
no longer able to sway in winter's frigid breeze,
clothed in mysterious dark shadows
like old monks in sleeping shrouds.
Like snow on a fragile rose petal,
pain, passion, and pleasure coexist.
So beautiful to observe
yet so cold to touch.
As the final curtain descends,
pretty autumn shades vanish
beneath a blanket of snow

.................It is winter!

POETIC ARTISTRY

A poet is an artist, constructing pictures with words
creating scenes without brush or canvas,
depicting whatever image the eye can find,
interpreting, expressing, creating.
A landscape captured in a sentence,
or an instant arrested in eternity.
Vocabularies as expansive
as any artist's gentle touch.

Words to equal art, poems without words.
Conveyance of spirit by means of matter.
Monet and Matisse, Keats and Kipling,
Turner and Tissot, Browning and Byron.
Expressions; one soul talking to another.
Life seen through a temperament.
Same pictures, different minds.
Dimensional, enlightened diversity.

Compositions you can walk around
or poetic visuals with no substance.

Listen to the heartfelt expression,
observe the poetic impressions.
See visions and dream dreams
knowledge made efficient by skill.
Study both narrative and verse,
painting scenery within the mind.
Quick sketches of thoughts
or feelings of the sublime.
With rhyme, the poet's palette,
words are the consummate art.

An artist's garden is a lawn of poems
captivating flowers in a painter's tone.
The ultimate of all pleasures,
figment of the imagination.
A walk in the garden
is where creativity dwells.

A poem is born from emotion,
bred by passion, mastered by knowledge,
attired by words, dressed with imagery.
The voice of the soul which the poet feels,
in silence, but with the touch
and instinct of the artist.

THE SUBLIMAL CHALLENGE

Without careers for once, but with things to do,
no nightmares or anger or the rattle of fears;
we'll ask how it can be that we are so happy,
happy that we are alive in a world
that isn't universally beautiful;
alive in a world that doesn't have to be.

With no answers, just ourselves and silence,
we'll listen for the lessons that wait to be learned;
the lessons that move through passing light
that unify, unite and bring peace
where others are as happy to be alive;
in a world that is after all, beautiful.

Without visiting stark and impoverished places,
you'll never feel the sea pulling you under,
swallowing up cries for help before they form.
Until you experience such places within you,
you will travel in a tourist daze,
oblivious of much that endures or destroys.

Without ever turning your head away from the light,
close your eyes, ignore the happiness inside,
take on board the subliminal challenge.
But beware - unless you are subconsciously vigilant,
you may prick the membrane of discrimination;
the thin skin between the haves and have nots.

IT MAY NOT BE THE SAME TOMORROW

The cool, calm, soothing breeze, which blows today,
may turn into a hurricane or a tornado.
It may not be the same,
causing havoc and chaos tomorrow.

The moon, which peeps from behind moving clouds,
may be obscured, and blacked out.
It may not be the same,
telling a different story tomorrow.

The stars, which appear to be singing a song,
may be hidden behind dark angry clouds.
They may not be the same,
not twinkling with a smile tomorrow.

The alluring clouds that move and swing in the sky,
cast shadows on the dancing leaves and trees.
They may not be the same,
forming ghastly new shapes tomorrow.

The mistle thrush and blackbird sing joyous songs
that welcome the blooming flowers.
They may not be the same,
not spreading their wings tomorrow.

The rainbow, a gateway of colours, bids farewell
to the migrating birds of September.
It may not be the same,
no longer visible after it rains tomorrow.

All that fills my heart with the beauty and magic of love,
makes my heart sing with happiness.
It may not be the same,
pleasing some other eye tomorrow.

But the joy and love they have all given to me,
enriches my mind and my heart.
They WILL be the same,
remaining there as a song for today and tomorrow.

BEHIND THE SMILE – LOVE

CANVAS OF THE SKY

How was it that initial gentle familiarity
lead to such intense love
drenched in swirls of passion?

There must be a reason why a whispered voice
soft, like a breathless breeze
attracts me like the mystery
of your fragrance.
A reason why your smile,
like the sun shining down
on a bright summer day,
replicates the golden softness of your aura.
A reason why your passion
sets fire to a tranquil sea
and your eyes shimmer down
like burning depths of allure.

Why, on cold nights does the whispered words
"I love you" resonate like a lullaby
in an operatic season of romance?
Loud enough to penetrate the darkness
of the heart's twilight
illuminating everything it touches
like a spark of golden moonlight.
The beat of my pulsating heart grows louder
and the moonbeams shine,
painting my feelings for you my love
in the canvas of the sky,
for it is abiding

TO LOVE

To love is to share but one life together,
to build special plans for two;
to work side by side
then smile with pride,
as over time all our dreams will come true.

To love is to help and support each other,
with smiles and occasional praise;
to take time to share
to listen and care,
in many tender and affectionate ways.

To love is to be with someone special,
upon whom you can always depend;
being there through the years
sharing laughter and tears,
as a true soul mate, lover and friend.

To love is to cherish many fond memories,
of moments we lovingly recall;
of all the good things
that sharing life brings,
no matter how big or how small.

To love is to make each other feel special,
endorsement of a love that's true;
like the words in this card
it is not at all hard,
with a loved one as special as you.

To love is to treat each other the same
albeit Christmas time is now here;
though I haven't kept score
I couldn't love you more
than I've loved you throughout the year

HOW DEEP IS MY LOVE?

The beauty of the lake, it is always changing
with the light, the weather and the season.
Yet each change holds a splendour all its own,
each day precious for its very own reason.

In sunshine, golden stars dance across the water,
moonlight shines a beacon in the peaceful night.
The wind causes whitecaps to erupt and roll,
while calm brings assorted reflections of light.

The water has a bright new costume each day,
variegations of grey, green, aqua and blue.
Though each view is different, the lake is the lake,
lovely in its every colour, mood and hue.

Thoughts of the lake remind me of you,
of my wonderfully loving partner in life.
Tranquillity, elegance, beauty and charm,
such a paragon of loveliness that is my wife.

Your love is my beacon, my star and my light,
all your colours and moods so precious to me.
The depth of my love, not unlike the lake,
runs so deep, it will live on for all eternity

WALTZ WITH ME FOREVER

Dance unto the light,
sway to the sounds of time,
watch the angels bright,
as they dance within your mind.

Waltz with me forever,
dance my lover and sway,
to beauty, to laughter, to love,
to another perfect day.

PARTNERS

You have an angel's face, a loving heart,
a peaceful, sunlit smile that lasts forever.
Like a dancing duo, of which I am a part,
never as one unless we are together.

I know there is a world beyond our love
in which such thoughts are merely poetry.
But thinking of you now, I can't remove
the glow that shines on you from inside me.

How happy life is when some tender feeling
like a glowing candle lights up one's eyes.
For all my life you'll be my heart's true centre,
dancing like the sun across my skies.

MY POEMS

Poems, for me redeem the passion of each moment,
sublime, yet gentle as the calm that quells the sea,
all those around us that have license to comment,
know quite well how good it is for you and me.

Poems, like love allow the rivers to run freely,
the tides to turn without the least regret,
the mountains to give way to time,
sincerely pleased with what the aeons will forget.

Poems, like love turn every moment to forever,
and every thing to unintended song,
and makes a worship out of all endeavour,
and through its music, undoes all wrong.

This poem depict what marriage is all about,
what being together as one really means,
a lifetime of love we will forever share,
both enjoying as one, life's myriad of scenes

LOVE GROWS

The beauty of a wife is not just in the clothes she wears,
or in the figure that she carries.
The beauty of a wife must be seen from in her eyes,
because that is the doorway to her heart,
the place where love resides,
where love grows.

The beauty of a wife is not just her mind and body whole,
or the thoughtful, adoring things she says
but is reflected in her soul.
The beauty of a wife is the passion she always shows,
the caring that she lovingly gives,
as each passing year
love grows.

A LOVE THAT MEANS SO MUCH

There's a special place in my heart
that only you can touch;
a place where you can see and feel
a love that means so much.

Throughout the day I think of you
in my mind your voice I hear;
I close my eyes and bow my head
in my thoughts you lovingly appear.

The way we adore and love each other
makes it tough for us to be apart;
so when I can't hold you in my arms
I hold you tenderly in my heart.

OUR LOVE VOYAGE

While we cherish the love we hold for each other
intense, dedicated, yet often joyously carefree.
We are the in addition a father and a mother
and for the lives of others we are their trustee.

Long may our love voyage continue, sweet and strong,
as our future journey holds the hopes of more than two.
I pray our life together will be happy and long,
until then darling, my love is exclusively for you.

WHAT DO I LOVE ABOUT YOU?

That sparkle in your eye,
the warmth of your skin.
Your breath on my neck,
that stirs me from within.
The touch of your hand,
the smell of your hair.
The naughtiness in your smile,
and just knowing you care.

Your kiss on my lips,
your body near mine.
The stroke of your touch,
that feeling divine.
That last cuddle at night,
a passionate embrace.
When you close your eyes
and I see love on your face.

Yes, my music of love
is the beat of your heart.
For as long as it keeps beating,
we will never be apart.
Your personality and charm,
and the magic of your touch.
It's for these reasons and more,
that I love you so very much.

THERE IS NO LOVE GREATER THAN OURS

Your smile awakens my soul,
as the sun awakens the day.
A kiss and my heart is yours,
it seems a fair price to pay.

Your touch arouses my senses,
as the moon arouses the night.
Hold me and win me forever,
in your arms all things are right.

Your heart endures all emotion,
as the sky endures all the stars.
Love me and we'll have eternity,
there is no greater love than ours.

I'LL ONLY STOP LOVING YOU

When diamonds fail to sparkle
and flowers cease to grow.
When thunder doesn't echo
and rivers do not flow.
When hearts no longer wonder
and hands are never held.
When smiles are only memories
and the truth always upheld.

When trees no long blossom
and stars you can't behold.
When autumn has no falling leaves
and winter isn't cold.
When time has no more tomorrows
and rainbows have no hue.
Only when I leave this earth
will I ever stop loving you.

A DOZEN ROSES

Twelve paragons of nature's true loveliness
each one elegant, majestic and tall.
Every bloom symbolic - a part of our life
in which friendship is treasured above all.

One rose means 'companion', confidant, friend
so rare and yet valued so much.
Another rose the trust that we have in each other
and a third rose depicts your gentle touch.

A rose for the generosity that is always present
and for the love and caring you always show.
A rose for the comfort and kindness given
when this friend feels dejected and low.

A rose for the humour that makes us both laugh
and which makes your eyes shine so bright.
A rose for the dreams we share with each other
as we snuggle up close late at night.

A rose for the tolerance and deep respect
we extend one to the other with ease.
A rose for the passion we stir in each other
and how effortlessly we are able to please.

A rose for your splendid and undying love
that has helped me in so many ways.
A rose for when you bring rays of sunshine
into my occasional overcast days.

The very last bloom stands out above all others
God's handwriting with petals unfurled.
For me this rose darling, epitomises you,
the greatest wife in all of the world.

MY VALENTINE

A word from you is like a spark of light,
that illuminates my soul
and just as sunshine revitalises my being,
it's you that makes me whole.

There can be no corner; no dingy, dark place,
your precious love cannot fill
and when those around us start causing waves,
you bring calm, almost at will.

When circumstances dictate an honest voice,
one of integrity, sincerity and truth,
you never back down but give it me straight,
of your courage that's living proof.

So thank you my darling for just being there,
for the love you bring into my life,
I hope in your heart you feel the same about me,
as it's no secret, my Valentine's my wife!

WE'RE STILL DANCING

You know how much you mean to me,
such bliss brings lovelight to my eyes.
You speak – I hear a symphony
and we will dance where the bluebird flies.

No other soulmate could there ever be
to settle deep within my heart.
And cherish its key eternally
knowing that we will never part.

You are my summer and my spring
such bliss brings lovelight, never gloom.
The sun shines, the birds sing
and we will dance where the roses bloom.

EVERY DAY WITH YOU

Some say the time for love is Spring,
as nature blooms and the newborn sing;
it is the innocent year's most early hour,
a time when seeds of want will flower.

But others claim that Summer's best,
the sun is high and world seems blessed;
when lovers greet a bright new dawn,
the opening page for a life reborn.

Still others think that it's in the Fall
young lovers should lay out their stall;
languishing under the autumn trees,
a lovers' course they chart with ease.

For some of those with a frozen heart,
cold white Winter is the place to start;
the lonely, lifeless snows they choose,
rejecting warmth, no love to lose,

For me sweetheart, the choice is clear,
it is every season that I hold dear;
it matters not what climate it covers,
since the day that we became lovers.

Winters that are cold, and summers hot,
as long as I'm with you, it matters not;
regardless of climate how could I be blue,
in a lifetime of love spent with you.

WHAT IS LOVE?

What is love, but an emotion,
strong and yet so pure,
nurtured and shared with you
every test it will endure.

What is love, but a force
to bring the mighty low,
a strength to move mountains
and halt time's ceaseless flow.

What is love, but a triumph,
a glorious goal attained,
the union of two souls, two hearts
one that angels have ordained?

What is love, but a work of art,
sculpted from a heart of stone;
a symbol of peace and tranquillity,
one of never being alone.

And what is love, but forever,
eternal and truly sincere,
a flame that through wax and wane
will outlive life's brief years.

So I'll tell it on the mountaintops,
in all places far and wide,
that love for you is my reason to be,
and I'll shout it out with pride

WITH WORDS ALL MY LOVE IMBUE

How can I make this time of telling special
when I tell you that I love you every day?
How can I tell you that you are my angel
when you are aware of that anyway?
I love you more on this, your day of birth,
than on the day we married, long ago.
Like a tree each year in height and girth,
my love has grown and continues to grow.
But each time our eyes join instead of meet,
it's as though the lights of stars and sun.
Join in me, a burst so bright and sweet,
it couldn't be contained by anyone.
And so as poetry it flows to you
that I may with words all my love imbue.

DIARIES OF OUR LIFE

Yes, my poems could be read in silence
but less poignant than when spoken.
But then my words, even if whispered,
will hopefully stir emotions for you within.

It matters not how one conveys what I have written
for my words are mere emblems, symbols, tokens.
Expressions of love that bear joint signatures,
passionately chronicling "Diaries of our Life."

My words applaud to the very echo your personality
so take a bow - let them become your legacy.
Words are not meant to be veils of secrecy
but are threads that weave life's rich tapestry.

When next you receive a bespoke love poem,
be glad lover, that you inspired its creation
For words not only pay homage to the present
they augur well for our future destiny together.

H.O.M.B.F

It's so hard to find the perfect breeze,
not blowing too hard or soft,
carrying the scent of beautiful flowers,
and moving the clouds aloft.

It's so hard to find the perfect sky,
that's clear and blue and bright,
carrying a sense of openness,
with geese and gulls in flight.

It's so hard to find the perfect night,
that's calm and quiet and still,
carrying a mood of tranquillity,
an expression of nature's free will.

But there is no perfection so hard to find
as the love that you extend
and none I'll ever treasure more than
to be the *husband of my best friend*.

A WIFE – SOUL MATE & FRIEND

A wife is the one who tells you the truth
regardless of any cost,
a wife will help you find all the things
that you didn't even know you had lost.

A wife seldom tries to put you down
or score points to make you feel small,
she'll smile and always comfort you
as together you can conquer all.

A wife is the one who will pick you up
when life is dragging you down,
a wife is the one who holds you at night
wearing nothing - not even a frown!

So when you think you're on your own
in need of a helping hand,
a wife has a pretty discerning ear
to both listen and understand.

And because the world is full of folks
insincere and who like to pretend,
you really are a lucky man if........
like me she's your soul mate and friend.

BIRDS OF LOVE

Cavorting together on a bright and beautiful day,
we see wild birds that seemingly never sleep.
Casting fleeting shadows on a field where lovers lay
before a scenic, mountain backcloth climbing steep.

Like the birds, these two have found joy in love,
a bond cemented by trust they will never forsake.
In unison, togetherness like those flying above
it is a picture of genuine true happiness they make.

They whisper softly, lovingly, reassuringly
saying how much pleasure to each they bring.
A young love that is visible for everyone to see,
a love which inspires those wild birds to sing.

A hill and a valley, a river, a forest and field
this world is such a glorious and wonderful place.
Today they decide their undying love will be sealed
committed to a new future they seek to embrace.

Nakedness, passion, abandon and pure delight
upon a tidal wave of emotion their love now rides.
Whether following a sign, an omen or a guiding light
love is consummated where true happiness hides.

Winter approaches and migrating birds spread their wings
looking down on a couple once unfulfilled and forlorn.
A parting chorus for a soon to be mother who gently sings
a lullaby to a wonderful new life that is about to be born.

EVERY MINUTE OF EVERY YEAR

I love you darling throughout the year,
not just upon Valentine's Day;
I cherish you when the flowers appear
in the months of April and May.
I adore you also in the summertime,
when the sun radiates much heat;
without you by my side every day,
my life just would not be complete.

I treasure you darling in the Autumn time
when leaves are turning to gold;
I loved you from the first moment we met;
and I'll love you when you're growing old.
I'll hold you close in the bleakest of winters,
when the frost, snow and ice appear;
in fact I'll love you darling all the time,
every minute of every day of every year.

MAURITIUS

This is a part of the world watched over by bold blue skies;
where the sun dances all day across the Indian Ocean.
Tropical foliage sways rhythmically upon the gentle breeze
like a vibrant and prismatic tabloid of perpetual motion.

Hotels concealed discretely amidst panoramic landscapes
look out over topaz seas and beaches of granular gold.
The perfect place for a honeymoon, a paradise on earth
one where treasured experiences cannot help but unfold.

CHRISTMAS MORNING *EN FRANCE*

Your footsteps penetrate my silence.
Elegantly and with such a slow and saintly pace,
they proceed mute and frozen
towards the bed of my wakefulness.

Pure being, divine shadow,
my cherished lover;
how genteel are your discreet steps!
All the love I can imagine
comes to me on those naked feet!

If, with your alluring and seductive lips
you are preparing to tease
the innermost depths of my being
with the sustenance of a kiss,
do not hasten that tender act.

Peace on Earth, a sweet peace
of being and yet not being.

This Christmas morning *en France*
I lie in expectation of you,
and my heart beats.
Its rhythm races at the sound
of footsteps neither mute or frozen.
Saintly footsteps my darling
that are yours alone.

Bonjour et Joyeux Noël ma femme

I SEE

I see a mountain somewhere near
the harbour of our love.
Where I can go sometimes to view
our marriage from above.

I see the vastness of the sea
outside our sheltered bay.
With boats like toys upon the flat
bare corrugated grey.

I see the shadows of the clouds
an archipelago.
That neither wind nor current breaks
nor charts of sea depths show.

I see the green of nearby hills
the gardens on our land.
The cultivated wildness
of nature shaped by hand.

I see the waves sweep up against
the rocks upon our shore.
The white spume leaping, oh, so slow
the heart awaiting more.

I see much peace and happiness
and passion shared for life.
Written in clouds across the sky
for a loving husband and his wife.

WILL I STOP LOVING YOU?

When tears never fall
and birds never fly,
when winter never ends
and children never cry.
When nights don't get dark
and the day is not light,
when forever finally ends
and our eyes have no sight.

When our ears cannot hear
and the grass never grows,
when silence is too loud
and the genius never knows.
When strength doesn't strengthen
and flowers never bloom,
when hearts can't be broken
and eternity is too soon.

When the wind never blows
and the rain is never wet,
when thunder can't be heard
and the sun just won't set.
When angels don't protect
and facts no longer true,
when life cannot be lived
and the sky is never blue.

When the truth is a lie
and the fake becomes real,
the clock shows no time,
and wounds never heal.
When enjoyment isn't fun
and bells cannot ring,
when races can't be won
and singers cannot sing.

When pain no longer hurts
and enemies never fight,
when rainbows have no colour
and wrong seems so right.
When all these things happen
when they finally come true,
only then my cherished one
will I stop loving you.

EVERY TOMORROW A VISION OF HOPE

Love knows no limit to its endurance,
no boundaries to excitement, no end to its trust.
To the world Angie, you may be just one person,
but to one person (me) you are the world.
Love is when I look into your eyes, and see your heart.
And, when you look into my eyes
you see that same heart.
As our marriage brings new meaning to love,
so our love brings new meaning to life.
Look well upon this day, your birthday
for it and it alone is life.
In its brief course lies all the essence of our existence:
the glory of marriage, the satisfaction of love,
the rewards of loyalty and the tranquility of understanding.
For some, yesterdays are but unfulfilled dreams,
and tomorrow an ill-defined vision.
But for us today, with life so perfectly positioned
every yesterday is a dream of happiness,
and every tomorrow a vision of hope.

MATRIMONIAL GARDEN

There is a light that shows me the way,
to a secret garden, with a fragrant bouquet.
And as I enter through its welcoming gates,
to savour everything that for me awaits.
I can't help but wonder why the light chose me
why fate gave to me the Gardeners key.
For whatever the reason, this much I know,
it is a gorgeous place where I love to go.
A garden that is full of life's delights -
of tenderness, affection and wondrous nights.

A garden in which to nourish my soul,
one place I can go and make myself whole.
Where the warming light beckons me stay
where every day it is Valentine's Day.
Sunshine, snow, wind, blizzard and rain
the garden's sanctuary keeps me sane.
Nature provides me with absolute proof
and time has shown me one simple truth.
That the light that shines from high above
is the nurturing light of your infinite love.

JUST AS....

Just as the meadows washed by rain
are re-lit by the arrival of dawn.
Just so our love, as we grow old,
will, each day, in our minds be reborn.

Just as the waves well up and cease
you are the anchor of my life.
Just as luck brought us together
not as mariners but as husband and wife.

Just as dawn heralds a brand new sky,
and whether it be sunshine or rain.
Just as every kiss, a brand new kiss,
is welcome again and again.

Just as I will always vow to love you
each and every day of my life.
Just come the morning that is our last
We'll die together as man and wife.

I KNOW I'LL STILL LOVE YOU

Should mountain ranges rise and fall,
or oceans drain and the forests die,
no force of nature, nor of time
could the bonds of love for you untie.

When ice-sheets crack or glaciers melt,
if tempests rage, or deserts grow,
poems of love will still get written,
to say how much I love you so.

No rupture in the world's true course,
no cataclysm of heat or cold,
can shift the axis where I turn,
or make our vibrant love seem old.

You are my sun, moon and my stars,
there's nothing for you I wouldn't do,
were this world we live in suddenly to end,
then in heaven I know I'd still love you.

A POET'S LOVE

What inspires these loving words we write,
that with burning passion our pens ignite?
It is a poet's love we proudly convey,
to express true love on Valentine's Day.

After careful thought and much reflection
we put pen to paper with deep affection.
While a bouquet of flowers just wilts away
the poems we compose are here to stay.

This poetry is meant to radiate and shine
an ode and a tribute to a dear Valentine.
Cementing a union that will forever endure
one of loyalty, friendship and love so pure.

Poetry, like your painting, is an *objet d'art*
conveyance of thought from mind and heart.
Though some view poetry as quite absurd,
our pens paint a picture with every word.

My undying love I have openly confessed
impassioned feelings tenderly expressed.
With words we poets hopefully impart
intimate thoughts from a sensitive heart.

I hope this poem is enchanting and divine
touching your heart with every new rhyme.
I've said it once but I'll say one more time
I love you to bits, you're...my Valentine.

74

I AM IN A NEW YORK MOOD

Some sing about Paris in the springtime,
others of Venice in the fall;
but what I've got planned for you this Christmas
will place New York ahead of them all.

A vibrant, pulsating, ever-changing Metropolis,
New York they say is larger than life;
with so many faces, facets and features,
instead of "Big Apple" why not call it "WIFE?"

Bridges, skyscrapers, taxis and subways,
ghettos, roof gardens and 'the Park';
a stunning and lively, half-mythical mosaic,
fraught with intrigue and mystery after dark.

The Bronx, Harlem, Manhattan and Broadway,
Coney Island, Central Park and Times Square;
although Christmas is still a long way off
I cannot wait to be taking you there.

IF I WERE A ROSE

Unfolding gently beneath
your loving touch.
(Sensitivity)
Buds turn into blooms
so radiant is your smile.
(Trust)
Each petal, individual yet one
sweet miracle of life.
(Bonding)
Sweet fragrant spirit touching
senses into life.
(Wisdom)
Giving beauty back to the universe
inspiring others.
(Caring)
We are hues of colour, yet transparent
in Spirits blossom.
(Integrity)

WITHOUT FEAR, WITHOUT REPROACH

Resonant whispers that awaken a silenced soul,
sweet caressing breath of virtuous divineness,
an essence of delicately dusted serenity,
hypnotic recollections that decorate dreams.

Calming salves that put body and spirit at ease,
furtive yet intuitive sense of understanding,
cherished and prized nobility of the infinite,
that feminine embodiment of all humanity.

The fountain of innovativeness and creativity,
the potency behind determination and resolve,
architect of charity, motivator of aspirations,
sphere of influence over developing thought.

A ray of sunshine greeting every morning dawn,
memories from multitudes of defining experiences,
an epiphany once seen only in the mind's eye,
the impetus that drives me to greater heights.

..... or phrased differently

The furtive but instant knowledge of mutual understanding
sweet moments when two minds morph into one,
essences of delicately dusted angelic solitude.
From the midnight easy ardent blushing of moonlight,
pins of light on the sable sky spell renewed hope
and warmed rains gently sooth away troublesome woes.
Each individual ray of sunshine from the morning dawn
delineates from a multitude of defining experiences,
an epiphany of that which is but a glint in the mind's eye.

TREASURE EACH DAY

The foundation of true love is loyalty and trust
and patience when things go wrong.
Of remaining true to your every word
for it is integrity that keeps love strong.
A wise old man once told me a story
about being respectful of your wife.
Because what you sew is what you reap
every day of your married life.

So what better way to live out your life
with both a wife and lover as one.
Not two separate, competing people
no battles to be lost or won.
For if your lover is also your wife
it's a good bet you will stay together.
You will be the luckiest man alive
a married life filled with devotion forever.

A happy marriage requires give and take
where the simplest things mean so much.
A smile, a nod, a squeeze of the hand
the pleasure of one another's touch.
There will always be times of hardship and stress
but mostly a relationship to treasure.
The envy of friends and those less blessed
a lifetime of much joy and pleasure.

Life is a rollercoaster with its highs and lows
hearts uplifted but occasionally broken.
But no problem is insurmountable if shared
by just being there - no words need be spoken.
Love will grow stronger through the years
but remember it passes us by very fast.
So build on the strengths that diminish the fears
and treasure each day as if it were your last.

BEHIND THE SMILE – GRIEVING

Son Jason: March 22, 1976 – June 23 2008

Jason's death represents a truly tragic story. Although a prolific songwriter, accomplished musician, DJ and radio presenter, he battled with depression for many years. He met with several psychiatrists and psycho-therapists during this time; he also had more than his fair share of anti-depressant drugs. For long periods he tried to blot out the really bad periods with alcohol. Over the last three years of his life he spent much of his time in America (his birthplace) but periodically came back to live with us when he just could not cope. He talked frequently about deriving no pleasure from life - nothing seemed to inspire or motivate him but that he was spiralling deeper and deeper into a black hole. He even talked many times about ending his life, as he could see no future - every day was a torment filled with pain and screaming in his head. But in his heart he knew it would destroy all of us if he took the easy (for him) way out.

We tried so many things over the years, and six months before he died, a great friend who is a recovering alcoholic managed to help Jason to stop drinking for a while. It was only then that we really saw the depth of his depression unclouded by alcohol. Even during that time no treatments seemed to work. However, in June 2008, we found a psychiatrist (the fourth over as many years) who Jason felt for the first time really understood him. Doctor Blacker assessed him quickly and decided his depression was very acute and deeply ingrained and that ECT plus a change of drugs was the best course of treatment. Jason was ecstatic that at last someone was on his wavelength and he was really looking forward to it, pinning all his hope on this fairly radical solution.

He was admitted into a private clinic on Thursday 19th June for tests but they were unable to set up the ECT for that Friday because they were short of an anaesthetist nurse, so booked it for the following Monday. They wanted Jason to stay in the clinic over the weekend to derive ben-efit from seeing the psychiatrist, receiving counselling and for them to monitor his new drug regime. Jason, however, was not happy about being an in-patient and also paying £650 per day for what he felt could be time just as easily be spent at home, until the ECT was started.

He was due back in on Monday morning. We all had a great weekend, with Jason being so full of hope and being the most positive we had seen him in years.

Angie went to wake him at 8.00am on the Monday morning (as we were planning to drive him back to the clinic) and found him dead. He appeared to have died from natural causes. Obviously the police arrived very quickly as did two paramedics and checked for signs of foul play, or an overdose (accidental or otherwise) or any other suspicious signs – but there was nothing.

It seems such incredibly bad timing - that we battled to get the right treatment for him for years - and were 12 hours too late. I think if this had happened months ago, we might have understood that Jason could not battle this disease any longer and may have taken things into his own hands. But to see him so uplifted and relieved at the thought there might be a solution to all of this, only to have his body give out at the last minute, seems so cruel.

Jason's funeral was on 4th July and was a very sad occasion for us all. However, afterwards we were all like-minded in our belief that it was conducted in a manner for which Jason would have been grateful, proud and just a little amused. The eulogy pretty much summed up his life, both the positive and the negative and the music we chose was comprised either of songs he had written and performed, or those he enjoyed listening to sometime in his life. We chose a coffin that looked like an old airline-packing crate adorned with an American flag. All of his friends were given a simulated airline sticker/baggage tag upon which they wrote personal messages and they were affixed to the side. The finished article resembled a crate that had travelled many times around the world. The sentiments expressed on those stickers/tags were truly amazing and really were a tribute to a lad who, despite his troubled years, had clearly touched the lives of many in a good and meaningful way.

The poems written during this time enabled me to exorcise those demons that kept telling me I had let him down and or that as a father I had failed. No matter how you try to reconcile things in your mind, the fact your son does not survive you, casts doubts on your own parenting. It is very true then, that writing was my catharsis.

Had we discovered **Depression Alliance** at that time, it might have resulted in a very different outcome. I say this not from conjecture or speculation but because I have met a number of sufferers since who claim that their association with this charity saved their lives.

COUNT OUR BLESSINGS

The physical form has died,
but his image is still alive.
We will cry over his death,
remembering all we shared.

The soul it rests in heaven,
the memory in our heart.
Let's count our blessings,
he knows how much we cared.

22/06/2008

IF...

If I can get through this sad day,
contain the pain inside of me,
no matter how heavy my heart,
or how dark the moment may be.

If I can but keep on believing,
what I know in my heart to be true,
then darkness will fade into morning,
and with this dawn a new day, too.

22/06/2008

LIFELINE TO SANITY

My soul drifts aimlessly in times of such sadness.
It searches tirelessly for the meaning of life …
Yet it finds no answers or direction.

My heart bleeds silently in times of such confusion.
It yearns to find comfort and understanding ...
Yet they somehow elude me.

My eyes seek out visions in times of such despair.
Staring endlessly through the darkness that envelops them …
Yet they cannot see the light.

My ears listen intently during times of unearthly silence.
Searching for familiar sounds to comfort and console ...
Yet they cannot penetrate the quiet.

My arms reach out frantically in times of such distress.
Praying for strength and compassion to embrace me ...
Yet they find nothing substantial.

My mind cries out desperately in times of such solitude.
Posing intense questions that demand insightful answers ...
Yet there are none to be found.

My hand reaches out in these times of such loneliness
It is held and I hear a familiar and calming voice ...
Angie, my lifeline to sanity.

24/06/2008

NON, JE NE REGRETTE RIEN (OR DO I?)

The rationale:

Had I known it was to be the last time son,
I'd see you walk through the door,
I would still have given you that fatherly hug,
but then called you back for more;
if I had known it was to be the last time son,
that I would observe you fall asleep,
I would have knelt down by your bedside praying,
the Lord your soul to keep.

Had I known it was to be the final time J'Ace,
that I would see your spirits raised,
never would I have foolishly built up hopes,
or the Lord above been praised;
if I had known it was to be the very last time
I'd be sharing a minute with you,
I'd have repeatedly told you "I love you son"
instead of assuming you already knew.

It is natural to believe there'll always be 'tomorrows'
to make good ones oversights,
and that each of us has plenty of time son,
to put this troublesome world to rights;
but had I known it was to be the last time J'Ace,
we would share another full day,
then I'd never have assumed there'd be many more,
and thus let it slip away.

..and the lesson to be learned:

Each of us assumes there is plenty of time
to say those special "I love you's"
and many more opportunities still lying ahead,
to ask those "Anything that I can do's?"
But just suppose, friends, that is not the case,
and today is all you're to get.
Why put things off for another day?
Those moments you might live to regret.

Tomorrows just cannot be guaranteed,
for both young and old alike,
so today may well be the last chance you get,
to hold a loved one tight;
it is easy to compile a long list of excuses
or reasons to do nothing today,
to prevaricate about those all important things,
we ought to take time to say.

Trust me – if you ARE one of those individuals
who puts things off for another day,
DON'T, for should tomorrow never come,
you will definitely regret the delay;
sorry that you didn't take time to deliver,
that precious smile, hug or kiss;
remorseful at not granting a special person,
what may be their very last wish.

Please hold your loved one close this day
and whisper tenderly in their ear,
tell them you love them very much
and that you'll always hold them dear;
take time to say, "I am sorry" "forgive me"
"thank you" or "it's okay"
and then if tomorrow sadly doesn't come,
you'll have no regrets about today.

24/06/2008

THIS OL' CRATE

Finally, at his journey's end, Jason can again dream,
destined perhaps for a Kingdom vast and pure,
where he can re-establish his lost self-esteem
and the mantle of achiever he sought to secure.

For this his final journey Jason will travel light,
gone the baggage of depression and despair,
he's chosen a flight path which for him is right
- let's hope this ol' crate will get him there!

LIFE'S GAMBLE - With God the croupier

Those aged persons who pass away
having lead a balanced and fulfilled life;
some highs, some lows, many happy memories
tinged perhaps with a little strife.
- dear God, that fair game of chance we understand!

But for those lost souls whose life ends,
troubled by dependency or depression;
no highs, constant lows, plagued with pain-filled days
in endless succession
- dear God you surely dealt them an unfair hand!

(02/07/08)

DJ TO THE ANGELS

The ones we love and lose never go away,
they walk side by side with us each passing day.
Unseen, unheard, but always quite near,
still loved, still missed, still very, very dear.
Jason my eldest, how I miss him so,
each day my heart breaks as I try to let go.
No matter how much and how hard I try,
it hurts me so much we had no parting good-bye.
So many special words I so wanted to say,
leave an ache in my heart that won't go away.

My memory still recalls great times gone by,
many treasured memories that still make me cry.
Friends all huddled round him, stories being told,
as they plot and scheme to find that pot of gold.
The wink he would give me, for a secret we shared,
despite his frustration, pain and despair.
He now roams the heavens, free of earthly pain,
DJ to the angels in the good Lord's domain.
A request for you son, sent up there to the sky,
may our love for each other never, ever die.

FACING A LONELY TOMORROW

When he wanted a friend to talk to
I always tried to be there.
When he needed a person to listen
he could rely on me to care.
Now he has gone I really don't know
just how I'll face tomorrow.
Someone please won't you help me
cope with all my sorrow.

Never doubt that I will ever forget
all the good (and bad) times we shared.
In youth the joy and trials of growing up
in later life the concerns you aired.
I treasure all the many memories
upon which I can now borrow.
Someone, please won't you help me
face a lonely tomorrow.

At times my sadness can be very acute,
but then his music fills me with pride.
If I concentrate and listen hard I hear
"Dad, my love for you never died"
and that's when I know with help
I really can face tomorrow.
Thank you son for really helping me
cope with all my sorrow.

(After Jason's cremation -July 2008)

THE SOLEMN MUSIC OF SILENCE

Tonight my heart tries to resurrect the lyrics of a song,
to create upbeat sounds in a silent life.
Taciturnity stays with me till sleep comes at last.
Sad but perhaps true, in times of grieving
the most poignant lyrics are wordless -
the solemn, pregnant music of silence.

FATHER ON EARTH TO ONE ABOVE

I despair at you, sovereign of the grave
that my son's life you failed to save.
Many heartfelt pleas fell on deaf ears
crystallising all of my deadliest fears.

My cries for help all seemingly in vain
agnosticism perhaps just cause for disdain.
What better assurance could you give
but to answer my prayer and let him live?

Grim reaper, withholder of his vital breath,
arbiter in this game called life and death.
The stake - yet another soul destroyed
laying waste a young life once enjoyed.

Much sadness cloaked by the vale of night
extinguishes forever life's flickering light.
Was the Devil responding to pleasures unrefined
or God's warm welcome for a moral mind?

Closed now are eyes that no longer weep
senses now bound in a never-waking sleep.
Anguished screams cease and sighs depart
gone the agony from one broken heart.

No reprieve then, for those who lost their way
he died; one more vassal of your sway.
Brutally severed another umbilicus of love
from a father on earth to one up above.

The ice-cold shell of his lost soul shall rise
beyond you, proud native of the skies.
For today my son leaves this earth behind
in his wake, more pain of a different kind.

This life that was wayward in many ways
now seeks peace and tranquillity where it lays.
Back close to nature his ashes are spread
with bluebells and dandelions for his bed.

Observe now, my softly-stealing tears apace
down this distraught mourner's sullen face.
As I look to where his now chilled ashes are laid
cast beneath an old oak's impervious shade.

*(Written after we scattered Jason's ashes under
an old oak tree in a nearby graveyard)*

LOVE CREATES MEMORIES

His death creates wounds no one can heal,
a lingering sadness, so hard to conceal.
Like a dagger in my heart no one else can feel;
misery, sadness – such an agonising ordeal.
I am merely human I'm not made of steel
so to preserve my sanity I tearfully appeal.

In front of his Maker I silently kneel,
praying for answers and for him to reveal.
Is it just a bad dream, for it seems so unreal
for us both to lose sons is so very surreal.
I think you'll agree Lord, tho' still a bad deal,
love creates fond memories no one can steal.

IT IS NOT EASY TO LET YOU GO SON

Now you have come to the end of the road son,
should I rejoice for a soul set free?
Or should I shed tears in my gloom-filled room,
which I know you'd hate to see?
I will miss you Jason, so very, very much
but not with my head bowed low,
for I'll remember the love that we always shared
making it easier to let you go.

Sadly it is a journey we all have to take
and inevitably we must go it alone;
it is seemingly part of some master plan son,
a final step on the road to home.
Although your departure saddens me J'Ace,
I am with those we both loved so,
who will share the grief and the sorrow I feel,
making it easier to let you go.

Who knows what lies beyond this life?
We can but listen to those who believe,
and if there is a God I hope he'll smile
and your doubting spirit he'll receive.
But just as in life you'll do things your way,
unlikely you'll just go with the flow,
you'll be treading a path that feels right to you,
making it easier to let you go.

Despite the many difficulties you faced son,
I never really doubted for one minute,
that given a period of good health and some luck,
the sky would have been be your limit.
So, as I try to rationalise my grief J'Ace,
and come to terms with this terrible blow.
A voice in my head says, "I am at peace Dad"
making it easier to let you go.

(02/07/08)

FOREVER YOUNG

Trapped for many inglorious years
within the memory of disbelief,
an uncharted path littered with obstacles
destination unclear, destiny uncertain.
But care not, there's nothing left to fear
for you Jason will be forever young,
always in the heart of memories,
lost of all grief, the final song sung.

Like an unfinished manuscript,
lost in the glory of all time,
the wisdom was there within your smile,
but none of us could fathom the ending.
Did you know; could you have told us,
what final chapter you had in mind?
For us, there within lies the mystery
the twist in the tail, an ending so unkind.

So we shed a smile, and grin a tear,
and thank God for the time we had;
we still see you through our misery
and we miss you, of course we do.
For you my son will be, forever young,
forever a talent and star bright,
forever in the heart of memories,
dee-jaying as usual, in heaven tonight.

(Written while compiling commemorative CD)

LEGACY

Music is the soundtrack of your life,
listening to it spurs memories
...that's when you fell in love
...that's when you passed GCSE's
...that's when you graduated.
It brings back memories
...of parties,
...of holidays,
...of your first job
when you fell in love (for real this time)
and got married.
Music, like a photo album
freezes moments in time
and certain lyrics
like faces
stay with you forever

(While compiling Jason's Commemorative CD)

WHAT IF?

While asleep last night, as I had always feared,
those damned 'What ifs' once again appeared.
Neither a nightmare nor a very nasty dream
just mental torture of what might have been...

What if the family had stayed in France
would he have then stood a better chance?

What if for schooling I'd made different choices
would we still be whispering in hushed voices?

What if my career had demanded much less
would things have resulted in far less stress?

What if I had spent more time with my son
would this agonising journey never have begun?

What if a home for his music he had found
would he be composing a chart-topping sound?

What if I'd never brought the family to Bath
would his life have taken a different path?

What if the doctors could have cured his fears
would we today be shedding all these tears?

What if their treatment could have eased his strife
would it have kick-started a brand new life?

What if the clock could now be turned back
would his life have taken a different track?

The dream finally recedes; as do all those fears
the questions stop and my brain again clears.
As the new day dawns and I feel less pain
I pray the 'What ifs' won't come back again.

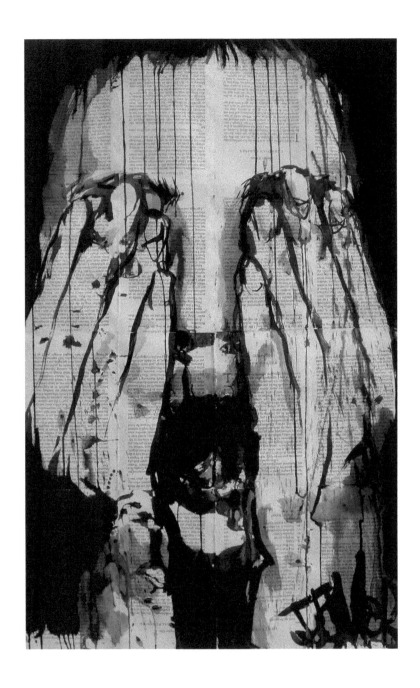

ILLUSIONS OF MYSELF

And so this very day it came to be,
a nightmare ending my worst fears.
As I look inward to the inner me
the world recedes; life disappears.

I remember the way it all began -

A proud father who cherished
something much more than this.
Not a young life that perished
for a reason which yet I miss.

My mind is angry, dark and deep,
such anguish I have yet to tame.
Before yet again I try to sleep
I must ignore this sense of blame.

Life will never again be as it was,
an anthem perhaps to parenting lost?
How many others feel the same,
or seek answers at any cost?

I remember the way it happened-

What was it that absorbed me quite,
that drowned my spirit; drew my breath?
Stole my senses, shut out my sight,
taught me grief and how to handle death?

With each and every awakening light
this pain lives with me deep inside.
Depicting the illusion of myself
and asking what I have to hide.

 (6 months after Jason died)

CELEBRATE OR MOURN?

Christmas is a time that families enjoy
happiness, laughter and many a new toy.
They praise the Lord and celebrate as one
for the birth of Jesus, his only son.

This Christmas concludes not the best of years
sadness, heartache and many tears
We question the Lord and mourn as one
at the loss of Jason our eldest son.

(Christmas 2008 – not quite the same!)

CAN YOU NOT SEE?

Because my face
creases with laughter
and my mind is often
steeped in song;
can you not see
I suffer greatly after
tolerating pain
so long?

Because my eyes
hide tears of sorrow,
you do not sense
my inner cry?
Can you not see
tho' my aching heart
still beats,
I might die?

FATEFUL DESTINY

A cold, damp and blustery morn
brings with it sad memories;
of a life unfulfilled, burdened, torn
... a flame extinguished.

Moments within moments flash clear
through tear-filled lashes;
has it really been another year
... of enduring sadness?

One day blurs into another
one heart beats slowly;
as air only serves to smother
...the endless hours.

He drifted so quietly away
I hardly noticed;
it was more than just another day
...a brutal awakening.

Glimmering ice, the winter's cold
has made me believe;
death, though it be so bold
...awaits dreamily.

Reaching out with guilt and fear
time erases dear memories;
my mouth moves, can't you hear
...silent screaming?

Misty colours fade from life's light
into dark - a quiet rest;
a loved one taken from my sight
...fateful destiny.

(A year after Jason's death)
23/06/2009

A SHADOW THAT DARKENS THE DAY

I am angry; the rage of insult furrows my mind
yet it is only an offense given to me by myself;
it is not from the mouths of others am I insulted
or that causes tears to trickle down my cheeks.

For I fear that I have been guilty of mistakes
whether real or imagined, avoidable or not.
Regardless of how others argue my innocence.
I am not very good at rationalising hindsight.

I try to shine like the advice of grace given
but memory and consequence rear their heads.
A constant reminder of what might have been,
a ghastly shadow that darkens the occasional day.

This shadow makes me doubt many of my decisions
that I might have done things differently or better?
What if I had put others before self, family before job,
put sports days and school plays before career?

Do all parents feel guilt or only those who've lost a child?
"What ifs" can torment the mind and torture the soul.
Yet I must exercise care—for the lines of memory run cold
and if criticism is due, no one but myself has that right.

Yes, I do have the right to degrade my every being;
those who argue with me are not feeling what I am feeling.
In their nightmares they are not seeing what I am seeing
or awake to that ghastly shadow that darkens the day

(Fifth anniversary of Jason's death)

Last night as I stared at the photo on the CD cover
I know the ending, what the final chapter holds in store.
Eventually I turn over, sad but at peace I sleep.
In a sweet maze of different dreams, I compose
a melancholy manuscript, a writer's goodbye.
(See next poem)

A WRITER'S GOODBYE

I dreamed of a punctuation mark, a full stop
so obscure its significance at first lost.
A subliminal termination of something,
very special and beyond words.
Bringing an end to the paragraph headed grief,
but a precursor to yet another chapter - memory.
In dreams how the mind distorts recall
like a muddled, jumbled manuscript;
memorability somersaults, recollections subvert,
pieces missing, falsehoods, a life not lost?

How much of memory is imagination
and if loss is in reality an absence,
why does it weigh so heavily?

As a writer, the analogy is of incorrect grammar,
punctuation marks in the wrong place;
a misspelled name emphasised in bold print,
underlined, highlighted bracketed
- a name that saddens.
The hand of a wife corrects, edits, re-writes,
words, any words to rise, rescue me
from this wait, this long silent loss.
Sadly we are both now different people,
new chapters of ourselves.

Sometimes I awake and still feel that grief
and my heart beats out its strange litany
of the enormously conceivable.
Like trying to catch the wind in a net
or weave a rope of sand.
Memories frustrate me until I become an instrument;
one in which anger rises up like thunder.
But the echo I hear coming back off the walls
is not thunder but my strangled, choked-up voice
quietly calling "Goodbye"

MY WORDS HIS MUSIC

Music was in his soul, it is his legacy
and my memory.
His music was love crying out to the world
and it remains within me as creation.
Music elevates human spirit to divine spirit eternally.
I do not need music for there to be poetry
but the music he wrote resonates within me
and the poems that I write in his memory
are more than just a dream.

Poetry is life to me and his life was music to my soul.
His world and my world circulated
to the beat of the music he made.
When I embrace the melody of music
I feel the spirit of words travelling in me.
What is music? Music is the rhythm of the soul;
it served as his motivation and inspiration.
What is poetry? Poetry is the rhythm of the mind;
it takes me to a world full of imagination
- and memories

In summary, music is Gods gift to the imaginative poet,
one who listens to the leaves whistle in the wind.
Every poem has a music of its very own;
lyrics are the story and music the song.
Are musicians then the poetic minstrels?
When I close my eyes and feel the rhythm of Jason's music
I dream that an angel of his music playing one of his songs
is somewhere near.
Music never dies. Poetry never dies
Sadly composers and poets do!

BANISHING DEMONS WITH WORDS

My inner self has found a way to communicate,
it is painting with the gift of verse.
I interpret and write about life,
about wonders of fragrant poetic offerings
versed in accordance with what I see and feel.
A mosaic of delirious euphoric visions
or the ignominy of despair and sadness.
It isn't all about just writing poetry,
it's often about banishing your demons with words.

Today my subconscious screams to me constantly,
loathing my cognitive presence.
I wrestle with traces of my past that pain me
or conflict with the person I seek to become.
Rebellious pieces of my psyche
rise up in solidarity with sad memories
- angst, anger, frustration, sadness, grief
But with the gift of verse, a catharsis,
a flower, a new life, peace aplenty.

When these rivers of words run dry
and that final creative block arrives;
when there is no more hideousness,
or secrets to share, reveal or unfold,
just a vast chasm of nothingness and emptiness;
then my final verse will have been written
and I will have reached that utopian moment;
a moment as pure as the one I am in right now.

Those who have known true darkness
can with words, find light in the deepest abyss.

Trust me, I know.

BEHIND THE SMILE – ENCOURAGMENT

DISTANT DREAMS.

Hope is analogous to a tuneful songbird
its bright, colourful plumage an aura of hypnotic hues
sitting on the boughs of your soul
singing a song.
The lyrics foretell of happiness
and the chorus of how good it is be alive.
How all the dreams we hold
in our hearts can come true.
What is life the songbird sings
but the chasing of distant dreams?

Look no further, the lyrics apprise us,
take time, stop searching.
Look inside your heart.....
for a dream is waiting there to encourage and inspire you.
Listen to your heart....
It encourages you to go forth without doubt and without fear.
Be guided by your heart....
for it senses the power of your dream;
the strength that it gives you
to find your happiness every day of your life.

Finally the songbird stops singing,
no longer sitting on the bough of your soul.

It has flown in search of more unhappiness
despair and unfulfilled dreams.
But the soul it leaves behind - your soul,
resides now in a place of utter perfection.
For your heart has picked up the birdsong;
a fresh beat, better tune with new lyrics,
describing not a dream but a reality - a perfect place .
A place filled with peace, tranquility and love.
A place where those distant dreams
held in your heart, can come true.

LIVE FOR TODAY

There'll be some days when the sun doesn't shine
when the skies are not radiant and blue;
when a great sadness prevails upon this earth
for which no solutions are apparent to you.
Don't let your enthusiasm falter or stumble
though life's steps may seem steep to climb;
try to stay on course and fight to the end
for not doing so would seem such a crime.

If dreams always turned out just as we wanted
like converting hard work into play;
all of our prayers would surely be answered
washing all of life's problems away.
A young life like yours would then be resolute
unaffected by wind, rain or storm;
whereas sadly in real life it's never that simple
as such miracles have yet to be born.

This Christmastime be thankful for your life
worry not which way the future will go;
enjoy this special time with family and friends
those who love you and miss you so.
Whether a future in America is meant to be
I simply cannot predict in this rhyme;
But I do hope this Christmas will be filled with joy
and that while here you'll have a good time.

106

A FATHER'S PRIDE

I remember it well son, when you were a boy,
always giggling and skipping while playing;
I knew then, you would bring us a lot of joy
and that you have, son, goes without saying.

Be it watching you playing with a puppy in the yard
or wiping tears from your tender cheek;
preparing you for a life that could be hard
in a world that is no place for the meek.

Your prowess as a sportsman was something to behold
and in rugby you scored a few tries;
dare I say it - there might have been one more
had that touch-judge closed his eyes!

In my mind's eye, son, you are a good friend too,
a son with integrity, character and pride;
so I hope you will keep on doing as you do,
making it a memorable and fulfilling ride.

Son, never attempt to compromise your heart,
stand up always for what you believe;
keep caring about others and do your part
- remaining honest, trying never to deceive.

I'm proud to tell the world you are my son,
one who is near perfect in so many ways;
what else can I say except when all's said and done
I will love you until the end of my days.

LIKE FATHER, LIKE SON

A saying I hear often is –
"like father like son"
a fairly obvious analogy
when all's said and done.
We model ourselves
on examples from our Dad
more often one hopes
for good than for bad.

From cradle to grave,
though a variety of ages,
fresh values are learned
at life's different stages.
Good role models
every young person needs,
for without it in life
a child rarely succeeds.

Just like a horse to water
fathers can but lead,
but none can dictate
if you'll fail or succeed.
If a father's behaviour
a son does imitate,
then a truism it is
"we get what we create".

BIRTHDAY BLESSINGS

Instead of counting candles son
or downing a dozen beers,
just contemplate your blessings
for twenty-nine great years.
Consider all those special folk
who love you, and who care,
others who've enriched your life
by just simply being there.

Think about the many memories
passing years can never mar,
so many experiences great and small
that have made you who you are.
This special day please celebrate,
keep your spirits up, and say,
"Instead of counting candles Dad,
I'll count my blessings on this day!"

IT'S A LOVE WITHOUT END, AMEN

There are times I know when you're feeling blue,
when you need a friend to help you through.
To make you laugh, and to make you glad,
bringing you happiness when you're feeling sad.
A sympathetic hand to dry away your tears,
the strength and support to overcome fears.
To ensure that today you can stand up strong,
when all about you seems to be going wrong.

Someone who will love you with all their heart
who's perhaps not first choice, but can play a part.
I know Dads can be difficult, grumpy and cynical,
calculating, questioning, challenging even clinical.
But one thing is certain and swear that it is true
a day doesn't go by when I don't think of you.
Because dads don't love their children every now and then
"It is a love without end, amen."

CREATE YOUR OWN RAINBOWS

Believe in your heart
that something wonderful is about to happen.
Love your life.
Believe in your own powers,
and your own potential
and in your own innate goodness.

Wake every morning
with the awe of just being alive.
Discover each day the magnificent,
awesome beauty in the world.
Explore and embrace life in yourself
and in everyone you see each day.

Reach within to find your own qualities,
amaze yourself and rouse those around you
to the potential of each new day.
Don't be afraid to admit
that you are less than perfect;
this is the essence of your humanity.

If necessary let those who love you help you,
trust enough to be able to take.
Let a little sun out as well as in.
Create your own rainbows;
look with hope to the horizon of today,
for today is all we truly have.

YOUR NEW FOUND MISSION

A friendly smile and a kindly wave
makes for a cheery disposition.
To cultivate happiness every day
must be your new found mission.

Hold only thoughts that serve you well
and banish all the rest.
They have no place inside your head
as you face this ultimate test.

Fight bravely on and steel yourself
for your goal is crystal clear.
One day you'll proudly tell us all
a new graduate now lives here.

BUT GETTING THERE....

Don't quit when life gets difficult
or when the going gets tough.
Don't quit over doubts and questions
for you're made of sterner stuff.

Don't quit when the night is darkest
for you'll soon be bathed in sun.
Don't quit when you feel you can't go on
when the race is almost won.

Don't quit when the hill gets too steep
for your goal is set quite high.
You will never be a failure my friend
....until the day you fail to try.

ROSEATE DREAMS

As the early morning dawn rises over the cliffs,
the earth around us awakens and comes alive,
showing off its beauty in a resplendent ray of colour.
My eyes linger on the cerulean ocean stretching out before me,
glowing vermillion in the rising sun.
Touched by a light summer breeze, wispy and cool,
my mind conjures up an exotic shore line
where I follow your footprints in the wet sand,
wondering whether the incoming waves
will caress or crash my roseate dreams.

The warm, summer breeze whispers seductively in my ear
and I feel a dual sense of both freedom and belonging.
As the gentle, rhythmic waves caress my feet
a soaring, heaven-kissing sunrise
sits now exalted supernal, high in the sky
and I thank the universe I am alive.
For there is no place I would rather be;
a perfect moment in a perfect place,
nothing but you, me and the sea
happy together sharing roseate dreams.

As laughingly we walk on down the beach
my mind again dips into the sea of ideas
and conjures up yet another thought.
Although threatened by the incoming tide
we playfully build a child-like sandcastle
together at the water's edge.

On the return journey I notice our footprints
have all been swept away
like tumbleweed in an old cowboy movie,
but that the waves have not touched our sandcastle.
I look out smilingly at the cerulean ocean
and once again a thought crosses my mind;
that castles of sand on the beach of love never crumble.
Tides from the sea of ideas only caress the depths of love,
so that happily ever after we live our roseate dreams.

LIFE'S WINDING ROAD

As you steer your way along life's winding road
many distractions may come into view;
if you're ever unsure where the road is going,
seek the road called "being true to you"
       and don't deviate from what you set out to do!

 Always remember just exactly who you are,
especially in times of hardship or fear;
never deviate, falter or consider giving up
but focus on the journey you set out to steer
       and follow those dreams you hold so dear!

You'll encounter many setbacks, even rejection
frequent frustrations, many failures too;
but you must overcome these bends in the road
to reach the heights you know you can do
       and realise those goals you hold so true!

While travelling remember to laugh and smile,
for not doing so is a high price to pay;
so wherever life's winding road takes you
make sure you have fun along the way
       and get the most out of life every day!

And for my sons Rory & Jamie,

Although we're not with you on your journeys,
remember that you're never alone;
we're never more than a phone call away
wherever it is you that decide to roam
       and there's a place in Bath called home!

BESTOW THE RICHEST OF BLESSINGS

I have the names of many folk
written down in a book
and when writing Christmas cards,
I open it and take a look;
and as I do, I realise,
those names all form a part,
not just of the book they're in,
but of my very heart.

Those entries record many people
who've crossed my path over time
and who in the years that followed,
became good friends of mine;
because once you've met some people,
the years cannot erase,
those memories of a kindly word
or of a welcome, friendly face.

Whether I've known you for many years
or simply just a few
in some small way you've played a part
in shaping things I do;
so, may the holy spirit of Christmas
that I hope forever endures,
bestow the richest of blessing
on the hearts of you and yours.

FRIENDS

As each of us walks the path of life
we meet new people every day.
Most are simply met by chance
but some are sent our way.

They become our treasured friends
whose bond we can't explain.
The ones who always understand
and share our joy and pain.

These bonds contains no boundaries
so, even when we're far apart
these special friendships comfort us
with a warmth felt in the heart.

This bond becomes a passageway
making distances disappear
and so, these friends, who've been sent our way
...remain forever near.

(To a friend in prison) 4/11/08)

AS EACH DAY PASSES

I shall not mind
the whiteness of my hair,
or that my steps
one day falter on the stair,
or what strange image
greets me in the glass
if I continue to feel,
as each day passes,
that on the hockey pitch
I can still kick their asses!

*(Birthday greeting to good friend and veteran hockey player
Richard Clarke who has since passed away)*

117

FRIENDSHIP

Friendship is a priceless gift
that can't be bought or sold,
but its value is far greater
than a mountain made of gold.
For gold is cold and lifeless
it can neither see nor hear
and in those times of trouble
it is powerless to cheer.

It has no ears to listen
nor heart to understand,
it cannot bring you comfort
or reach out a helping hand.
So when you ask God for a gift
be thankful if he should send,
not diamonds, pearls or riches
but the love of a true friend

(To a friend in prison)

LOOKING IN THE MIRROR*

When you're lucky enough to enjoy good health
but feel angered by what's come your way,
then go to the mirror and look at yourself,
and see what that guy has to say.
For it isn't your father, or mother, or wife,
whose judgmental test you must pass,
the person whose verdict counts most in your life
is the guy staring back from the glass.

It is to him you must answer, never mind the rest,
for he'll be with you 'til the very end,
and you'll have passed your most dangerous and difficult test
when the guy in the glass calls you 'friend'.
There are people born bright and others real dumb,
but we know you are an intelligent guy,
yet the man in the glass will think you a bum
if you can't look him straight in the eye.

You can fool the whole world down the pathway of years,
getting pats on the back as you pass,
but your final reward will be heartaches and tears
if you've cheated the guy in the glass.
You've now days-a-plenty to engage in a stock take,
to reflect on just what you have done,
for if as we suspect this was just one terrible mistake
the guy in the glass and you will be as one.

*(*The original of this poem was scrawled on the walls of death row in San Quentin prison and thought to be anonymous. In fact it was written by Peter "Dale" Winbrow Sr (1895-1954), titled "The man in the glass" and was published in 1934*
I have adapted the words for my friend in prison 09/11/08)

BEFORE YOUR TIME IS THROUGH

All too often we don't realise
what we have until it's gone,
seldom taking time to say
"I'm sorry - I was wrong."

Sometimes it seems we hurt the ones
we hold dearest to our hearts,
allowing many foolish things
to tear our lives apart.

Occasionally insignificant things
cloud one's busy mind,
and then it's usually far too late
to see what made us blind.

So be sure you let a loved one know
how much they mean to you,
take that time to say the words
before your time is through.

Be sure that you appreciate
everything you've got,
and be thankful for the little things
in life that mean a lot.

(To Margaret Pearson who has cancer; re: Daughter Michelle)

MOTHER OF TWO DAUGHTERS

You will both think of Vi with love today,
but that is nothing new.
You both thought about her yesterday
and days before that too.
You may both think of her in silence
or occasionally speak her name.
Because all you have left are memories
and her photo in a picture frame.
But memories are great keepsakes,
it means you're never far apart.
For while God now has her in his keeping,
you each have her in your heart.

(To Bobbie & Vicki at the death of their mother Violet)

MAKING A WISH

The sunlight is as passionate as flowers
bordering the sidewalk of a song.
Clouds shape its golden apertures for hours,
shifting with each breeze that comes along.

The day becomes a mustard-coloured sunbeam
falling through the window of your smile.
Mystical images, like attendant spirits,
sit upon your windowsill and linger awhile.

How beautifully the choir of the mountains
sings to its rapt audience of sky blue.
As dancing down a corridor of fountains,
we toss in coins and make a wish for you:

FRIEND FROM A BYGONE ERA

Roads in life are often confused and twisted,
strewn with damaged dreams and lost hope;
often, what remains is a bleak, empty space,
and with little direction, we but barely cope.

In the profound darkness and eerie silence,
only faint memories of joy can be heard;
in a life overrun by difficulties and stresses,
we strain to understand but a single word.

It is in those times, when our faith is fading,
when no question of life makes any sense;
we wish a lost friend would call our name,
saying what once was broken only has dents.

Out of that silence, out of a night once dark,
a friend does appear from shadow to sunlight;
laughter abounds and memories are relived
as old friends from a bygone era reunite.

Now we're stronger, no longer are we silent,
our voices are a chorus; futility is on the mend;
blessings abound because I've once again met
dear Margaret - my long time, long lost friend.

*(Meeting Margaret Pascal, old friend from 30 years
 ago who has Cancer) 26/10/08.*

MY OLD FRIEND (I)

Hearts filled with laughter
and eyes moved to tears,
with memories so vivid
transcending the years.
The words of compassion
and actions so kind
the sun smiles down
when old friends come to mind.

I've counted my blessings
and shuffled my dreams,
and sung to the music
of deep forest streams.
Searched for a safe haven
where hearts are twined,
like deep in my soul,
when old friends come to mind.

An old trusted friend
one guide on my path,
both confidant and critic
yet so good for a laugh.
Now it's your birthday
I know you won't mind,
me writing this daft poem
to an old friend I call mine.

(To Richard Clarke on his birthday 9/07/2009

FRIENDSHIP THAT NEVER ENDS

To Alan we must finally say goodbye
so let's celebrate his life - not cry.
As friendlier man as you'll ever get
who in our hearts we'll never forget!
The angels came to take him home,
now we are left on earth to roam.
His time was long, yet seemed too short
so to memories now we must resort.
For everyone here he had a smile
and he loved to sit and talk awhile.
Now in our hearts Alan still lives on
until our time on earth is gone...
Then once again we'll join our friend
in a place where friendship will never end!

(Goodbye to friend Alan Symons, who died yesterday)

LIGHT A CANDLE

Light a candle Maureen, it will help remind you
of your time with Alan here on earth,
and as the flame flickers, remember him
- his kindness, his goodness, his worth.

Glow long and bright for Alan little candle,
ensure that his memory will never die,
and Maureen, as you see his rugged face in the glow,
shed a tear, say a prayer, then smile your goodbye.

(To Alan's partner Maureen at time of his death)
13/02/2011

MY OLD FRIEND (II)

My heart once filled with laughter
now my eyes are moved to tears,
memories that are so vivid
transcending many years.
Words often filled with passion
and actions cool and kind,
for me the sun smiles down
when this old friend comes to mind.

(You know) I've counted all my blessings
and shuffled all my dreams,
he's been a listener and a counsellor
when life's not what it seems.
When searching dark places
the light has always shined,
like a beacon in my soul,
when this old friend comes to mind.

We both loved our local rugby
and shared good times at Bath,
always a great host and raconteur
who enjoyed a really good laugh.
But now my mate has left us
so I hope that he will find,
some comfort in this poem
from this old friend he's left behind

(Death of my good friend Alan Symonds
Adapted from an earlier poem written
to Richard Clarke)

DARK AND LONELY DAYS

Sadly Anne, I can say that I do know just how you feel
that your hurt is great and it will take time to heal.
Is it possible for such a wound to completely ever mend
when you've lost your souls mate, child or good friend?

Though there are very few comforting words I can say
please know that I'll be thinking of you every day.
My thoughts will be with you, in small and simple ways
for I know what it is like – those dark and lonely days.

Those around you will keep saying "Time will heal"
but please call me and talk about anything you feel.
Though it is impossible for a cousin to end your pain
we can hold each other's hand down Memory Lane.

(Death of cousin Anne's husband Mike 27/09/10)

127

LOVE LOST

As I lovingly look into the old lady's eyes,
she smiles at me warmly, a little surprised.
Sitting there quietly in her comfy chair,
a pretty young nurse calmly brushing her hair.

She now looks very thin, so frail and weak
and clearly has difficulty trying to speak.
It saddens me greatly to see her this way,
no future to speak of, nothing left to say.

She now lives her life very much in the past,
the present for her goes by far too fast.
Her two loving daughters she greets with glee,
but it's clear she no longer remembers me.

I wish I could bring her sound body and mind,
if only there were a key that I could find.
To reactivate her memory, to break this trance
and to again see her laugh, sing and dance.

But sadly it has gone, that sparkle in her eye,
she knows before long she is going to die.
She has come to terms and ready to let go,
the girl I once loved many decades ago.

*(Dedicated to Margaret Pearson, the girl to whom
I was engaged in the 60's who died in
2012 of cancer)*

IT'S HARD TO FIND...

It is very hard to find the perfect breeze,
one not blowing too hard or soft;
carrying an aroma of scented flowers,
and moving soft, white clouds aloft.

It is very hard to find the perfect sky,
one that is blue and clear and bright;
portraying a sense of real openness,
one with wild ducks and geese in flight.

It is very hard to find the perfect night,
where calmness and tranquillity surround;
one portraying an air of celestial quiet,
one in which fond memories abound.

Real perfection is also very hard to find,
even perhaps in a long time friend;
but I treasure the years we've been mates
and truly saddened they're about to end.

(Visiting friend Richard Clarke who was then critically ill and who has since passed away.)

THE BIG NINETY

When just a kid you were probably told
that reaching thirty was very old,
but then forty and fifty came very fast.
and sixty and seventy you soon passed
so your definition then, of getting old
changed repeatedly as the years rolled.

You probably thought then, it was weighty
when you celebrated reaching eighty,
but the years they kept coming apace
which is more than most in life's race
I bet you are now feeling mighty
to have reached the magic age of Ninety

(Happy birthday to my Aunt Connie)
12/2/09

WHO WE ARE TODAY

Come, Connie let us enjoy autumn together,
walking slowly through fallen leaves,
gazing through weary eyes
at the golden hues of distant landscapes.
Our steps are shorter now and we walk a little slower
as our warm days have all but come to an end.
Let us sit for a while and admire the view
and talk of those bygone summers past.
It has been a long and tiring journey;
that winding road from childhood innocence,
around mid-life corners
to a destination that is not too far away
possibly around the next bend.

In another age times were tough, life was hard
but then love was wild
as were thoughts and actions too.
Where have they gone, those good ol' days?
Sadly our memories of beautiful tomorrows
are now buried in fog-bound yesterdays,
trapped between here and some distant place.
Alas Connie, our winter will soon be upon us
with frozen reflections of old faces, bygone ways
and shadowed remnants of past life.
But, let's take pride and comfort
in who we are today
and think less about who we were yesterday.

*(Written after receiving a photo of Aunt Connie on her 95th birthday,
in Feb 2014 an old people's home and not at all well)*

THAT LONELY STREET

She treads wearily a lonely street
trying hard to fight back the tears;
kind nurses massage her swollen feet,
while doctors calm ever present fears.

Reflecting on life with a grateful heart
she refuses to countenance grey;
her asking us if it's not time to depart,
we praying for a peaceful way.

A quality life has forsaken her
as the pain they try to quell;
yet loving memories will comfort her
for deep within her heart they dwell.

So she'll keep on walking a lonely street
until a greater power calls her away;
so Lord with faith and hope I ask,
send an Angel Vivien's way

Each one of us knows her time is near
and soon you will take her home;
guide her gently to your Heavenly Kingdom,
where other Angels like Jason roam.

When she crosses over and steps into the light
when she is happy and free from pain;
we know that she'll do as she always did
- watch over us until we meet again

(Written after my last hour with Vivien 25/02/2013)

THE ONE WE CALL MOTHER

I wonder if there are Angels right here on earth,
teaching us values and encouraging self worth,
who guide us through life with wisdom and light,
steering us from evil and telling us what's right.

Who stand by our side when things get rough,
who teach us in bad times we need to be tough,
holding our hand through those formative years,
laughing in happy times, but then sharing our tears.

This person was sent down from the Lord above,
who he pays not in wages, but with eternal love,
her mandate is confidante, teacher and protector,
who when her job's done, we'll never forget her.

For her there's no halo, silken wings, or special place,
only rays from God's love lighting up her face,
this angel I'm talking of can be replaced by no other,
she is God's gift to us all - the one we call mother.

*(After listening to eulogy at Viv's funeral it brought back vivid memories of my
own dear mother . . . bless her)*

A NEW DAWN

A gentle breeze blew across this land
reaching out to take Vivien's hand,
floating on those winds the angels came
calling my mother-in-law by name.

Angie & Mike sharing sadness and tears
but also loving memories from many years,
the joy of her love and a life well spent
but now to God's Kingdom their mother is sent.

Today she has boarded that heavenly flight
a first class seat towards celestial light,
a dark day for those who mourn a life gone
but for Viv in heaven 'tis but a new dawn.

26/02/2013

THE WIDOW

She, unaccustomed to company
but from her husband;
an exile from delight
lives coiled in a shell of loneliness.
Then death intrudes from its holy temple
shock, realisation and fear
come into her sight
but liberate others into her life.

Attention and solace arrive
and in its train come ecstasies;
old memories of pleasure
ancient histories of pain.
She recoils at the tragic loss,
embraces new company
striking away the chain of fear
from her soul.

She is weaned from her timidity
by the flush of new light;
we dare her to be brave
and suddenly we all see.
That love costs all we are
and will ever be;
yet it is only our love
which will set her free.

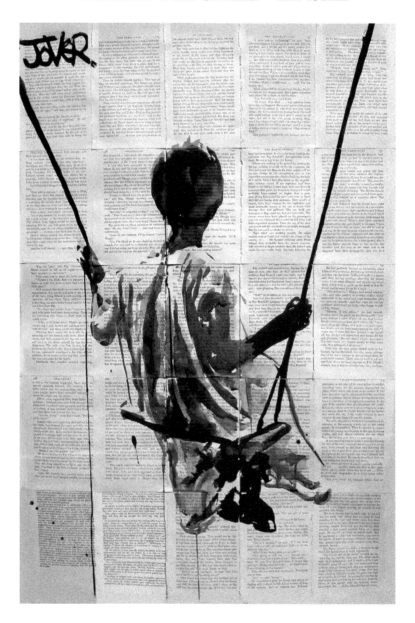

A LIFE THAT STARTED LONG AGO

Eve, may this very special August day
overflow with much love and peace;
as you thank God for his grace and mercy
because his wonders for you never cease.
Each life you have been blessed to touch
should remind us all to persevere;
for your commitment and loyalty to God above
gladdens hearts and minds, that's clear.

The unwavering strength that you possess
a devoted Christian in all that you do;
revering the One from whom you're made
ever faithful, ever loving and ever true.
Celebrate and enjoy this special moment
of a life that started long ago;
with a brother who loves and adores you
even more than you already know.

THE RHYTHM OF YOUR HEART

Like the tide, life's emotions constantly drift back and forth,
activated it seems, by winds of change that silently call.
Two hearts synchronised like the melodic rhythm of the sea
in unison beat and rise but mysteriously, never fall.

Sand and shells drift and shift underneath the surface,
each one moving separately and at its own pace;
but, in time they come to rest, content and at peace
relishing new experiences which for them are taking place.

From a far off distance we see in the mist of the sea's dew
a future of true understanding granted by the Lord above.
My sister and her soul mate discovering in each other
a warm ocean of happiness that is surely true love.

LET'S SING TOGETHER UNDAUNTED

Eve, I wish for you the most wonderful of birthdays
such that on this very special day your soul will sing,
heralding the brotherly love this message conveys
and the glad tidings these words hopefully bring.

Understand this silly, sentimental fuss I am making
for, like you I am touched by a love only we know.
You, a sister who gives so much, should now be taking
every reciprocal love and affection life can bestow.

Let our souls rejoice for the years we've been granted,
for each blessing bestowed; each child, girl and boy!
Offer thanks for receiving all the things we've wanted:
each victory, each pleasure, every happiness and joy!

Even if occasionally by dreams or memories you are haunted,
forget and sing, for on this special day you must not be blue!
No matter the aches and pains let us sing together, undaunted,
because on this special day Eve, I send my love to you.

A GIFT THAT MEANS SO MUCH!

He brings you joy in wonderful and mysterious ways
that only your heart Eve, can fully understand.
The feelings he evokes when his eyes meet yours
I suspect are almost more than your heart can stand.
Like a babbling brook, miraculously winding its way
through a magical, mystical forest slowly to the sea.
You look up in awe to that same creator and ask
"Is this another of your miracles happening to me?"

The stars in the sky spell out to you his name,
pushing back clouds that might try to move in.
They shine down brightly, regaling in your happiness
as if even they too wish not to lose sight of him.
No doubt Eve, he only has to whisper your name
and your kind but fragile heart skips a beat.
Hopefully, with reassuring and tender words
all your troubles and fears are put to sleep.

While in his company I sense you are engulfed
by the most beautiful, warm and wondrous light.
It's as if before him, life was shrouded in dark
a darkness akin to the dead of the longest night.
But, once again, as you gaze into this man's eyes
you will feel your heartbeat quicken, as does mine
when I hold my wife in my arms, tell her I love her
and pray it will last until the very end of time!

EVIE – A BIRTHDAY TREASURE

God gave a gift to the world when you were born -
a person who loves and who cares,
who sees a person's need and fills it,
who encourages and lifts people up,
who spends energy on others
rather than herself.
Someone who touches each life she enters
and makes a difference in their world,
because ripples of kindness flow outward
as each person you have touched,
then touches others.

Your August birthday is so very special -
it should be celebrated by everyone.
Maybe a national holiday should be declared,
because you are a real treasure
for all that you do.
May the love you have shown to others
return to you, multiplied,
I wish you the happiest of birthdays Sis,
and many, many, more,
so that others have time to appreciate you
as much as I do.

SHARING SMILES

Between us Eve, there are many miles
but, no reason we can't share our smiles.
Although not physically there, it's true
our hearts have travelled to be with you.
We hope good things will come your way
as you enjoy another Christmas Day

BEST WISHES FROM A THOUSAND MILES AWAY

On this your birthday, my dearest sister
I pray that all your dreams will come true,
a day that I hope will be filled with much joy,
a few gifts and some loving too.

On the day we all commemorate your birth
you'll want someone special to embrace,
sadly, since I am thousands of miles away
your son-in-law will have to take my place!.

Future years of good health and happiness
filled with many more years of laughter,
that is the gift we pray God will give you
and a future that is happy ever after!

GIFTS I WOULD PUT UNDER YOUR TREE

If I could be in Westport on Christmas Day
there are so many words I'd love to say.
However, most of them I've already said
so perhaps I would leave a few gifts instead.
Eve, the gifts I'd leave beneath your tree
are not the kind that you can touch or see.

Not wrapped in paper that's bright and gay
but gifts to bless you each and every day.
A brother's friendship warm and true,
is definitely a gift I would leave for you.
Also happiness, good health and much cheer
to keep you smiling throughout the year.

The gift of peace that comes only from God,
with a prayer to guide each path you trod.
And if ever your heart should lose its song
I'd leave the gift of hope to cheer you on.
These are the gifts I'd put under your tree
With love and kisses from Angie and me.

BROTHERLY LOVE

Let's look back on our unique relationship this Christmas;
over six decades of sharing our ups, downs, joys and fears
albeit many miles apart we can boast of a very special bond;
one that continues to grow ever stronger through the years.

We have both been and always will be there for each other,
honest, open, loving – no need ever to embellish or pretend;
this Christmas poem then comes from a very, special place;
a place in my heart reserved for you, my sister and my friend.

SEASONAL MESSAGE TO DISTANT FRIENDS

So, what is it we should love about Christmas;
should our delight reside in just things?
Or are the feelings we get deep down in our hearts
the real gift that Christmas brings.

It's a time for reassuring those whom we love,
across the miles we're thinking of them too,
taking the time to say thanks for the joy
that comes from having true friends like you.

We all know it's not only at Christmas time
but throughout the entire year too,
that the joy and happiness we give to others
is the joy that comes back to you.

For the more time we spend in caring and giving
to the poor, the lonely and the sad,
that reciprocal warm feeling of caring my friend
goes a long way to making US feel glad.

Christmas then is filled with so many emotions,
but for me friend the very best of all,
is contemplating those who are dear to me,
and the memories for me they recall.

Taking time to think about those whom we care
about those who we are today thinking of,
it's why this heartfelt greeting to a real good friend
is sent with sincerity, friendship and love

BEHIND THE SMILE – ANGST

THE ADDICT

Silence and misunderstanding wreck youth
they feed on loneliness and create a ghastly void.
Grey shadows haunt and torment and torture
as one more teenager is stricken and destroyed.

There is no sound of laughter or happiness here
as another youngster threw in the towel today.
Sombre and melancholy moods decay the soul
while inept politicians simply hope and pray.

Emptiness builds its home in this lost soul
in this person, this child where hollows have bred.
Where a deepening sea of despair consumes
and eats away at every connecting thread.

Anger and confusion feed like savages inside,
where the last vestibule of hope remains.
Destined to walk through life less ordinary
alone, exiled, different and disdained.

(Written after a visit to Clouds House Drug & Rehab. Centre)

YOUNG HEROES

What world is this where children fight,
murder, slay and maim with might?
Frightened, angry, warlike, proud,
liars, thieves - they boast out loud.

Stained teeth, small beards, tall and thin,
noses sharp and sun scorched skin.
Their youth a litany of barbaric scenes,
no understanding of what life means.

Butchers of children, women and swine,
all young heroes 'til they step on a mine.
No medical help so they die in pain,
lost souls forgotten; sacrificed in vain.

144

THE OLD MAN & THE BOY

Said the little boy, "I sometimes dribble."
the old man nodded, "Yeah, me and you."
The little boy whispered, "I wet my pants."
Laughed the little old man "I do that too."

The little boy looked up with dampening eyes,
he said looking sad, "I sometimes cry."
The old man smiled taking the boys hand
saying "Don't be ashamed son, so do I."

"But worst of all," the little the boy sighed,
"People ignore me, I might as well be dead."
The boy felt the warmth of a wrinkled hand.
"I know exactly what you mean," the old man said.

THE ANARCHIST

Asked to engage in talks and to avoid confrontation
we dance around the festering splinters of fate,
inheriting issues we never sanctioned or solicited,
a legacy festooned with reasons to despise and hate.

Genetics are what make people exactly who they are,
with every pair of eyes comes a different shape.
Preservation of the *status quo* versus exploitation;
what constitutes progress to one, is to another rape.

Chances for happiness will come in different guises
as we reconcile state of mind and state of being.
Were the generation before us really that uncaring
or simply intelligent but not really thinking or seeing?

One day I hope to wake and find I've been dreaming,
just a morbid play in which we are all required to act.
Accepting that the world really is beyond redemption
and my generation is happy to accept the fact.

But if I wake and find life is as it was in the dream
it will act as a sultry reminder of what we all knew;
that unless we engage in civil disobedience and confrontation
the essence of that morbid dream will come true.

WHAT DOES IT TAKE?

It takes strength to be tough.
It takes courage to be gentle.

It takes strength to conquer.
It takes courage to appease.

It takes strength to be certain.
It takes courage to have doubt.

It takes strength to fit in.
It takes courage to stand out.

It takes strength to feel a friend's pain.
It takes courage to tolerate your own.

It takes strength to endure abuse.
It takes courage to prevent it.

It takes strength to stand alone.
It takes courage to lean on another.

It takes strength to give love.
It takes courage to be loved.

It takes strength to survive.
It takes courage to live.

IMAGINE

Most of us can only imagine, what it's like to sacrifice
How it feels to go without, what it takes to pay the price
To offer some of what you have, to others with a need
Most can only imagine, for we're motivated by greed

Most of us can only imagine what it's like to be alone
How it feels to be rejected or get by on your own
Never to share a secret, feeling empty deep inside
Most can only imagine since for them it's about false pride

Most of us can only imagine what it's like to be abused
How it feels to lie awake feeling angry, tired and bruised
Having no friends to turn to, filled with rage one can't release
Most can only imagine as the majority of us live in peace

Most of us can only imagine what it's like to live with pain
How it feels to wake each day knowing treatment is in vain
Living a constant nightmare that nothing else can parallel
Most can only imagine what must really be living Hell

BELEAGUERED SOUL

Insomnia is the plague of yesterday's night
that haunts even unto the morning's day.
The state of a conscientious active mind
passing time in meaningless shades of grey.

Insomnia is a miserable world without colour,
without conventional or interwoven seams.
Beleaguered by problems as yet unresolved,
an inability to resurrect past dreamt dreams.

Insomnia is a distorted web of mangled art,
the Dali or Picasso of human emotions.
Craving a shawl of melancholic mist and silence,
yet plagued by untimely thoughts and notions.

Insomnia creates a strobe of distorted pictures,
flashes of faces amidst lightening and thunder.
A colourless tapestry of scars unyielded,
echoing throes of once peaceful slumber.

Insomnia weaves a tapestry of ups and downs,
disjointed thoughts haunting the faintest sleep.
A spur that makes man struggle with destiny,
gruesome memories making eyelids weep.

Insomnia can question even the purest of minds,
as feigning bravado, you dive into the awesome deep.
When guilt and humiliation tear at your very soul,
you pray the fruit of your errors you shall not reap.

Insomnia can be like a tsunami of mental debris,
memories swirling and flooding like a thinking quake.
Dark thoughts constantly prowling the shades of night,
stalking a beleaguered soul until it's finally awake.

THE EVIL WE COUNTENANCE

Insanity is not in itself tantamount to evil
but evil is always insane; is always sheer lunacy.
Evilness is no joking matter, nothing to laugh about
whereas insanity can often generate a smile.
Were we to consistently mock the imprudence of evil
then surely we would deny its power over us;
we might reduce its influence in today's world
and hopefully tarnish its appeal, its allure.

Throughout history it is the wilful and insane inaction
of those who could or should have acted;
the indifference, the widespread neurosis
amongst those who should have known better.
It is the silenced voices of justice and virtue
absent when clearly it mattered most;
minds focussed on less important issues
that made it so easy for evil to exist and triumph.

Apathy is the glove in which evil slips its hand
like a heavyweight boxing champion.
The strength of evil makes violence seem beautiful
compassion and kindness seem ugly and weak.
Insanity endures when men fight to cure evil with evil
but the rules of this game render it impossible to play;
because life itself is never good or evil
simply the place for good and evil to exist.

World leaders continue to countenance much evil
in the illogical belief good will come from it.
It is insane to think they can take good from bad,
yet insanity is seemingly the only yardstick
by which those who should know better, rule.
Aggression and self-besot to them seem beautiful
whereas compassion and understanding weak.
So, today the place for evil exists and triumphs still.

SYRIA

TV screens depict a patchwork of pitted, scorched earth
and the faintly luminous outline of derelict buildings;
there exists an eerie space between light and dark,
one of faint shadows stirring with abandoned hope.
The bland quality of this near desolate moonscape
enigmatically shrouds many blackened, sinister secrets,
much like a ghostly, colourless tessellate
at the bottom of a badly damaged kaleidoscope.

All weary of age and damaged by unseen scars
Syrians cry out for peace and resolution;
an end to this sick, ghostly screen of war
and the putrid, bitter suffering on those it inflicts.
A collective shame unwashed in generations
promulgated by selfish insane men in power;
mass graves and mutilations are harbingers
of these mindless, seemingly endless conflicts.

An entire civilisation of broken, distraught, souls
suffering daily physical, mental pulsing pain;
hearts immersed in lonely, sultry darkness
their once bright sunshine now turned to shade.
Damaged hearts and minds in ravaged bodies
all victims of an ugly, endless struggle;
millions wind-shivering in fearful silence
as all their hopes, dreams and futures fade.

NICOTINE HELL

Like an azure-blue apparition it drifts around the room
seeking a safe haven, a silent refuge.
An ocular spectrum floating across a thick silence
that is hanging in the air.
Stealthily it tendrils up from the glowing end in spirals,
writhing in serpentine patterns toward Nicotine Hell.
It is the calling card of the environmental nihilist,
the badge of the anti-social renegade,
the pollutant maverick who cares not,
who inhales those ominous fumes
that waft on the breeze.

The ephemeral pleasure of watching tendrils of smoke
permeating somebody else's space,
sucking in the pure air that others must forfeit.
He is a self-delusional misfit in a fool's paradise.

Huddled in groups just yards away from the establishment exit,
lit cigarettes emitting dusty clouds into the atmosphere.
Like schoolboys gathered outside the headmaster's study,
they inhale, exhale, cough and stare at the ground,
avoiding the steely glare of the sad
but healthy conformists they will never become.
You are either a smoker or you are not - there is no in between.
If you diligently worship at the nicotine altar,
you greatly improve your chances of early ascension
to the great world of dark that lies behind all human destinies

The Grim Reaper solemnly rubs his hands together,
encouraging you to light up another as he opens wide
the rusty coloured gates to Nicotine Hell

NICOTINE QUEEN

She holds a lipstick-ringed, filter tipped fag
between ugly brown stained fingers and, antithetically -
beautifully manicured and painted nails.
Observing sullenly the grubby pavement
blackened by ground out dog-ends
like confetti littering the street with anxiety.
Inhaling smoke, exhaling isolation and loneliness -
emptiness fills her heart as smoke fills her lungs.
The cigarette that is drooping from her mouth
she might think forms part of her beauty,
but it is a beauty she is subconsciously smoking away.
What isn't inhaled impregnates her clothing and sours her hair.
The white mist coming out of her blood red lips looks magical,
but the mix of smoke and nicotine twists and constricts her lungs
coating them like soot in a chimney or scale in a kettle.
She lights another to raise her spirits but
her heart turns black with the nicotine that revives her.
Soon her lungs won't rise and fall as mechanically as they should;
smoke is slowly cremating her for it is all smoke
and no mirrors in the throat of eternity

BEHIND THE SMILE – SHAME

OBSERVE THE PLASTIC FLOWERS

Look through the nursing home window,
observe the plastic flowers
swaying to a ceiling fan breeze.
A sad old man, wheelchair-bound
who for hours stares out of the window.
He sees a car park and undernourished shrubs,
motor cars and bicycles rushing by;
they keep him company
along with the faded draperies.

Suddenly he's become a slave to nostalgia,
a victim of disjointed and withered memories.
See the photographs on his mantle shelf;
notice how they stare back at him
with abstract smiles saved only for the elderly.
His medals displayed in a cracked glass case,
testament to the sacrifices he made.
Valueless in the balance sheet of today;
a symbol of history best forgotten.

I suppose everyone has their own life to live,
busy dealing with their own problems,
no time for compassion or sympathy.
Surely he'll understand
that no one now wants to look into his world,
not even to just share a thought?
They claim to have no time to visit,
although they know he is still here,
alive but very much alone.

(Written after meeting a WW2 veteran)

LONELY HERO

He sits there alone, staring out of the window
hoping that today he will see someone,
but alas today is no different from the others
for when night time falls no one has come.

For him now, days and weeks go by languidly
not unlike a slow motion instant replay,
a war veteran is he, now old and feeble
for whom isolation is now the order of the day.

Will this poor old war hero die here all alone
without any of his beloved ones near?
It is hard to imagine what he really thinks
as he wipes away yet another lonely tear.

We're told he fought for his county and won medals
and how he really worked hard all his life,
but now sadly he is confined to a wheelchair
reminiscing about his children and his wife.

"If only" he says, "they were alive and could be here"
those special loved ones he held so dear,
if only he could once again feel their tender touch
and just once more their voices he could hear.

His contentment would at last finally be complete
he would not at all be afraid to say goodbye,
but he fears deep down inside his heart
that in this nursing home, alone he will die.

His life seems to have gone by so very quickly
and tomorrow or the day after, he may be gone.
Will anyone really miss him or say thank you
to our lonely hero in that dingy nursing home?

(Written after meeting a WW2 veteran)

BYGONE TIMES

His outward energy and enthusiasm are bewildering,
the lines of age in his face are as young as mine.
His looks remind me of winter on a lovely spring day,
his mindset and disposition the epitome of the benign.

In conversation he constantly refers to bygone times,
mis-filed and confused in the aged tendrils of his mind.
Vague vestiges seemingly trodden by all of humanity,
are just excerpts of life and death inexorably entwined.

Sadly in his mind kindred vistas are deceptively adrift,
vague plans and promises recounted and reviewed.
Panic and then plight threatens his sensing thought,
before reality rudely awakens a once dormant feud.

Lurking in the hallways of his confused, tortured mind,
ghost-like, uniformed shadows loom most nights.
There is no safe place for our war veteran to hide,
with memories of old comrades his tortured soul blights.

Life for this old soldier is an evanescence of experience,
a mix of fate and fantasy, much sadness and little mirth.
Perhaps an old soldier's destiny is determined in the womb,
because in reality the cause of his ultimate death is birth.

*(This poem, Lonely Hero and Observe the Plastic Flowers were all
written after visiting a nursing home and meeting a old, lonely WW2
veteran)*

THE HOMELESS

When daybreak heralds the opening of a weary eye
and the sun gradually rises high up in the sky,
I set off from my home, an appointment to keep
in the heart of the City where the homeless sleep.

They sit huddled in doorways, so frail and so thin
because nobody cares or invites them in.
Passing alcoholics who've clearly lost the plot
I glimpse an abused child that time has forgot.

I pass a tall Cathedral where people are singing
and above their head church bells are ringing.
All oblivious to the strife that is raping their city
translating calls for help into accusations of self-pity.

Where's the good Samaritan; doctor, medic or nurse
with the skills and training to put right this curse?
Are they too busy focused on needs elsewhere
or have they joined the ranks of those who don't care?

Many politicians have walked these streets before
why can't they resolve things by changing the law?
I wonder if at night they have guilty nightmares
featuring sad, sunken eyes and desperate stares.

The streets are crowded with life's hopeless cases
with misery and pain etched deep in their faces.
Each new dawn brings with it suffering and pain
one of fighting for survival before starting again.

TORTURED LIVES

When no one takes the time to listen and learn
or bothers to express or exercise concern;
when we're so pre-occupied we cannot see
there is an underlying problem with humanity.

Whether it's a friend or stranger that cannot cope,
when they are on the verge of giving up hope;
by making their day even a little bit brighter
the burden they carry will appear much lighter.

By brushing away all their sadness and tears,
or helping to calm their very worst fears;
by building up confidence in place of doubt
it will certainly illustrate what love is about.

As attention seeking souls plagued by anger or pain,
who look like they're tormented or going insane;
as abysmal stories of tortured lives unfold
they're desperately in need of a hand to hold

If we give time to someone's suffering today,
their troubles will lessen and might fade away;
as a message of caring and of love we send
a one-time stranger might soon call you friend.

RUPERT

Sitting, like a blank canvas on the easel of life
is the portrait of a young and confused man
so distant, so distraught and troubled.
How can anyone penetrate the mood,
address the need, caress his wanton spirit?
He sees himself as a spent part of life's toxic waste,
harbours a desire to step off the world,
to escape its ugly, uncaring inhabitants
from choking him to death.
Yet somehow, somewhere deep within
his sunken soul is a desire
to carve out a future for himself.
He eulogises about a past now alien to him,
using words that paint a picture
of sunshine, animals and simple things.

The battle against his poisons were tortuous,
the scars, both mental and physical still visible.
Feuds, friction and abysmal bad luck
although behind him, are still causing anxiety.
But now he has a guardian angel on his shoulder,
one to care, to chase away the need,
to paint a different but realistic picture of the world.
A world he once knew before he became a sunken soul,
one to which he must now reach out and embrace.
Across virtual reality still many words of love,
tenderness, sincerity and of encouragement,
words of understanding and purpose,
yet with an abruptness that gives him a choice -
"Lie down my friend, be defeated and die"
or "rise every day with newfound optimism and live".

My *raison d'être* is uncomplicated but sincere;
give something of yourself, anything
to help those going down the same road as did Jason;
a long, winding, unmade and uncharted road,
a bizarre cul-de-sac with no turning circle;
a dimly lit, poorly sign-posted dead end.

With help, Ru can complete his journey safely get back on that straight and narrow road
build a life, avoid more pitfalls and pot holes.
With love and understanding as his driving companions
his body, his mind and his soul will be cleansed.
He <u>will</u> start every day with newfound optimism,
blossom like a flower in Springtime,
grow and flourish, ending each day
bathed in the glow of success, he will live.

(My thoughts after being introduced to Rupert who has
suffered many setbacks in life and for whom drugs, abuse,
being sectioned and two attempted suicides are his
calling card)

164

LOST TOMMORROWS

Our ancestors would stand in voiceless fixity
and gaze upon the decimated world
we are rapidly creating.
They would see landscapes that bleed solitude
like a wounded, weeping heart.
Once green and wonderful forests devastated,
fields, pastures and valleys ravaged,
rivers and streams polluted.
Creatures scarce and wild pay the price.
as one by one they vanish from the Earth.

Our ancestors will, out of the chill of marbled grief
weep for all those lost tomorrows.
Astonished by the risks we have taken,
numbed by grief for what is gone.
How precarious our destiny if we continue,
can we not learn from where we've been
as we stand wide-eyed, upon new shores
and look at what we are passing on?
How fragile is the legacy we are leaving,
how sad we have fallen out of love with our Earth.

Only when the horizon embraces lush valleys
and clear, azure waters feed the artist eye.
When we espy the beauty of butterfly wings
and see clearly the wild flowers blooming,
feel raindrops falling and smell the perfume inside a rose.
When we hear the calmness of clear blue skies
and feel the power of snow peaked mountains.
When white-capped oceans are alive again
and sea creatures fear not man's refuse.
Then, only then, can the bountiful Earth find love.

DEPRESSION – LIKE DUSK INTO NIGHT

A sad, under nourished flower exposed to insufficient light
will struggle to grow normal and may barely survive.
If unattended it fades and dies like dusk into the night
whilst dominant species nearby flourish, prosper and thrive.

This is not unlike many human souls struggling to cope,
battling the same odds as the flower wilting in the dark.
Without encouragement or understanding they'll give up hope
not wishing to face a life that is joyless, soulless and stark.

They ask pitifully - how can a fire be lit if there's no spark,
for without hope or prospects, the soul will waste away?
Much like the crest-fallen flower floundering in the dark
the depressed soul struggles to survive yet another day.

There must be help somewhere for those whose world is grey,
whose torment and sense of desperation is rife.
Without help and renewed hope their soul will waste away,
and bring to a premature end yet another sorry life.

How sad to hear that a living soul would rather be dead,
not unlike the flower that is deprived of natural light.
Both feel so low they give up the fight and with drooping head,
slowly fade away and die . . . like dusk into the night.

DEMENTIA

With assertive gentleness she caresses the strings of life
with the bow of tolerance she has used for years;
as the dust lingers more on the floor than the case
where forgotten she had once carried so many fears.

Raised to be frugal and chaste with an eye that searched
for everything wholesome, virginal and plain;
knowing each new day deprived her of many delights
with subtle nuances unappreciatively ordained.

Then there was the fog so thick she couldn't cut through it,
carrying a cold so damp it just crept into her bones;
diffusing light like a protracted eclipse of the moon,
creating shadows that obliterated all hues and tones.

Confused and disorientated she barely clings to sanity,
now hearing voices but without seeing a face;
she feels rain that she professes to touch and taste,
proclaiming a fear that it will flood this place.

The call of the morning sun perhaps gently reminds her
of the window that once opened onto better days;
days before she'd fallen into the uneasy malady
she describes as her latent and manifest malaise.

We all hope one day she'll feel the taut strings untighten
and experience summer days unspoiled by driving rain;
when once again like the fluttering of a bird's wings
she'll caress the strings and play life's sonata again.

RETIREMENT

Ahead of him there are new pathways to explore
as the future reaches out and beckons him
toward uncharted time.
He steps past memories and longings to reach out.
Life, no longer prescribed, is unclear,
verging perhaps on the surreal.
Days go by and he finds himself in a new reality,
an unhurried place of happiness and calm.
He senses the fragrance of freedom,
the air of pause.
In the once turbulent waters of life
there is now a tranquillity
he has never known.
So he smiles at the voyage ahead
and re-charts his course.
He cannot live in the shadow of regret
and not see what is right in front of him.
His life is now all about the present,
not meant to be over analysed.
Like doors opening up to new freedoms,
he can grab the handles, turn them,
or let them go.

DEPRESSION

Depression, a malignity that ends so many lives,
purveyor of loneliness and mental voids.
Grey shadows haunt, torment and erode
the ability to cope with the lives it destroys.

Emptiness builds homes in these lost souls,
beleaguered beings where self is dead.
Where a deepening sea of hopelessness
destroys sanity and mental thread.

Panic and confusion like a cancer inside,
until nothing but an empty shell remains.
Destined to leave this world misunderstood,
alone, exiled, different and disdained.

Listen closely, for there are tears being shed here,
another tortured soul has given up the fight today.
Sombre, melancholy - mind decayed by fear,
gone the will to hope and dream and pray.

THE ALCOHOLIC

No one suspects the false smile he is faking,
or notices his hands, how much they are shaking?
His mother and father claim they know him well,
yet neither sees inside his crumbling shell.

"I'm fine", he whispers, his sadness unknown,
"Please leave me to deal with my anguish alone.
I've hidden it from you for most of my life,
I've managed so far to deal with my strife."

They accept his excuses as being quite real,
"No one has to know of the pain that I feel".
He keeps it inside; thinks no one can see,
But while he fools others, he can't fool me.

PAYING THE TOLL

How tragic you look spaced out on your trip,
fighting for survival clearly losing your grip.
How sad to see you lying on the floor,
incoherent, vomiting yet pleading for more.

Your raving suggests you're messed in the mind,
rejecting any help of a remedial kind.
How pitiful you look begging for more coke,
blinded by white powder and chemical smoke.

Surely you must realise you are slipping away,
that really you must halt this damaging way.
How can I help you hold on to your life,
to stop all your suffering, torment and strife.

How can I stop you from selling your soul,
buying new needles and then paying the toll.
If to drugs you bow down, to drugs you will fall,
the stage being set for that last curtain call.

I am truly saddened by a life that's been wasted,
that none of life's pleasures you've ever tasted.
I heard on the grapevine that you chose to die,
and to a drug dealer you bade your last goodbye.

SPEAK UP

You don't trust politicians, now that's a surprise
their aimless rhetoric and never ending lies;
so, rise up together and speak with one voice
because votes mean the power to influence choice.

Speak out for the poor who can't make ends meet
or the unemployed who hang out on the street;
or the homeless folk who live out and about
don't speak in whispers, speak up and speak out.

Fight against pollution of lake and of river
boycott corporations that fail to deliver;
fight to preserve your forests and your streams
protect the wildlife that feature in your dreams.

March upon Parliament with placards and songs
you possess the power to right many wrongs;
don't be content until you reverse the trend
that is careening your world to a premature end.

Think of the future, young citizens of this Earth
fight to save this planet for all you are worth;
don't tolerate mediocrity because you are young
write what you think, let your pen be your tongue.

*(Written after attending a seminar at the university given by graduates
about how we are destroying the planet)*

I SAW A SOLDIER CRY

He stood there with his gun held high
watching bombs fall from the sky,
shrapnel ripping bodies apart,
tearing a hole in his caring heart.
With disregard for sanity,
in a senseless act of lunacy,
he sees two children fall and die,
the day I saw a soldier cry.

Raising his torch he reads the sign,
a few miles only from the enemy line,
homes and houses now violated,
by hatred and evil orchestrated.
Hounds of Hell have been released,
so he and his men must kill the Beast.
I saw his head droop, shaking "Why?"
the day I saw a soldier cry.

With grime on his face tears fall like rain,
anger building up like a hurricane,
circling the enemy with whirlwind force,
they will kill the evil at its source.
To deliver the ultimate in recompense,
to those who prey on innocents.
But I'll never forget, I know I cried,
The day I heard that soldier died.

(Written after watching a TV documentary about war in Afghanistan)

BEHIND THE SMILE – HOPE

WHEN I WRITE

Not everything on the spectral canvas is joyous;
wars, poverty, suffering, pain and death.
These conjure dark, sinister, grief-stricken,
even demoniacal pictures.

When I write about tragedy or death,
I want you to sense dark clouds descending
like a shroud enveloping a corpse.

When I write about poverty, pain and suffering,
I want you to feel hurt, sympathy and compassion;
shed the occasional tear, offer comfort.
Make sacrifices, donate to charity,
give thanks, be grateful and pray -
"there but for the grace of God go I"

In stark contrast, serenity and tranquillity
should abound when I describe the stars;
the solace and comfort of their soft glow.
Then dawn, an exhilarating burst of beauty
burns a bright light through a cobalt sky.

Tears of joy should stream down your face
as I describe magical sunrises and sombre sunsets;
it should leave you breathless in awed elation,
as I describe a rainbow's hues from silver to scarlet.

Each season offers a new literary opportunity,
each word a new beginning, a new creation.

Sometimes I write of love and I feel love coming back
because my readers are a joy in my life.
We share emotions like we share the seasons
so for us the spectral canvass is always joyous.

LIFE'S STRUGGLE

I used to complain when outside it was raining,
when it was so cold, no one ventured on the street.
When storm force winds blew a hundred miles an hour
their anger and ferocity blowing me off my feet.

When these vicious elements electrocute my senses
and lightning carves the sky with angry streaks.
When broken tree limbs shatter picket fences
and raucous thunder renders a disarming speech.

When the waters rise and churn around me
and rivers, battered and broken, admit defeat.
Every morsel of my soul craves shelter
as I battle elements that refuse to retreat.

This my friend is the fragile life that we inherit;
these are the numbered days that mark our place.
The Earth (and life) can be so intimidating
yet I rejoice when each day shows its face.

(Written after severe floods hit the south west 31/01/2014)

WILL COURAGE RETURN?

Who will ultimately survive this imperfect world -
the estranged lover, whose love has died,
or the angry rebel who trains children to fight,
or the waif who grew up and lives on the streets,
or daughter who ran away in shame for her deeds?
Countless lives, unimaginable stories;
tragedy, grief, sadness; happiness, joy and love,
each soliloquy emitting its own verbal fragrance.
There was a beginning and there will be an end,
but what will befall us in between, my friend?
Will life grow and meanings surface?
Will we find peace, will courage return?

Who will ultimately survive this imperfect world –
triumph in life's lottery as the moments unfold?
Humanity begrudgingly sharing this space, this age,
like angry misfits, sharing in this societal charade.
Conforming to convention, blinded minds,
attempting to control others' opinions.
'Freedom' born inside, is contested openly.
Can we free ourselves, free our minds,
transform the world, change the vision?
If hope blossoms, love can chart a course,
as life grows, meanings surface,.
Peace reigns... and courage returns.

HOLD ON TO YOUR DREAMS

Remember, how you face up to life today
affects all of your tomorrows.

That turning down the wrong road
is only part of the journey
and that finding the way back
is your real challenge.

Remember that if you keep love
close to you own heart,
home will never be far away.

There will be expectations not met,
promises lost, tears shed,
and sadly - moments of real despair.

Remember, however,
to be grateful for the sunshine
and to find hope in the rainbow.

Remember to laugh from your soul
and always hold on to your dreams.

(Happy birthday old friend in prison 29/01/09)

THANKS MY FRIEND FOR EVERYTHING

Indignantly displaced, the moon now solemnly resides
along with darkness, recoiling behind distant gates;
both forced to retreat in the wake of a crimson tide
as sunrise, through closed shutters slowly penetrates.

The heavens bow and the stars slowly begin to disappear;
charcoal skies turn grey, then disperse to a pale orange hue.
Suddenly all the stars have gone and the sky is quite clear
for that pale orange hue has given way to a wondrous blue.

A new dawn breaks and bathes the world in wondrous light
like a golden dome erupting, a radiant lava of orange and red.
Once more the world awakes from the spectre of eternal night
encouraging every living creature to leave its cosy bed.

Every somnivolent trapped in the deepest of dreams it frees
and every living being is forced to shake off sleep and rise.
The warm, welcoming sun shines down from above the trees
to the relief of all the flowers, the birds and the butterflies.

We humans awake more slowly but likewise greet this dawn
for it heralds a new day and all the adventures it might bring.
Again, as we count our blessings, grateful this day to be born
we look skyward and say - thanks my friend for everything.

WHAT IS HOPE?

Hope is a beacon, a bright shining light
designed to keep darkness at bay.
Hope is akin to a gentle breeze
bringing relief on a hot summer's day.

Hope is all about staying the course
when the going gets tiresome or tough.
Hope is looking for more things to do
when you think that you've done enough.

Hope is dreaming of things still undone
looking forward to a new tomorrow.
Hope is about holding your head up high
when inside there is fear or sorrow.

Hope is the opposite of a heavy burden
carefree and light as a feather.
Hope is the catalyst that gels and bonds
keeping loved ones and friends together

Hope is something we all must hold dear
it is both ubiquitous and free of cost.
Hope is crucial to our very survival
it is something that must never be lost.

With hope comes a smile, radiant and bright
replacing tears in the corner of an eye.
For hope is truly a wonderful thing
one that must never be allowed to die.

(Written to a friend in prison 05/06/09)

WAKING UP FROM A DREAM

A distant chord of optimism, like a lilting melody
slowly embraces my consciousness.
The rhythm of my heart beats like a bass drum
and my pulse throbs within my veins like a metronome.

Against a lurid psychedelic backcloth, shadows sway
to the shifting tide of loud, manic music.
The room engulfed in bright and vibrant hues
creates an energy field amidst a mass of cavorting bodies.

The crowd, bursting into song, captures the lyrics in unison,
the words rolling off their tongues, note by note.
Waves of music flow through their veins and minds,
the graduating leaps and bounds of plagal cadence.

Like a symphonic tsunami it finally takes control,
my head is pounding at the cacophony of sound.
Enigmatically my mind goes into slow motion delirium,
enlarging imagination's boundaries into infinity.

Abruptly I wake in a cold sweat to life, to reality,
exhausted , aware vaguely of a pounding in my chest.
Doubts, unfulfilled dreams and broken hopes,
a faded future, lost but never found.

Sometimes nightmares don't end when we open our eyes,
they simply become real.
But hey, my head doesn't hurt - I don't feel anything,
the music has stopped and so has everything else.

A BOOK REVIEW

He leads us through a complex plot,
its disparate elements he holds
in perfect balance.
This psycho-thriller carves a distinctive patch
on the map of contemporary crime writing,
like finding a Mondrian in the attic
- surprise followed by ecstasy.

He dares the reader to accept his clever misconceptions
moulding them into a crime story
as chillingly compelling
as a plane crash.
Characters are vulnerable personalities
with a plethora of doubts and anxieties
who have experienced the downside
- just like us.

His stories are strong, taut, full of suspense;
with well-oiled plot mechanics,
edge-of-the-knife dialogue
and explosive bursts of violence.
Polished and primed
like settling behind the wheel of a classic car
masterfully crafted, immaculately engineered
fast, fluent and exciting
with pace and assurance
- that never lets up.

He writes about real people
in real landscapes;
physical, social and psychological.
Gripping and powerfully atmospheric,
drenched in mystery and twisted desire;
excruciatingly suspenseful,
rich in character;
- it engages the reader at all levels;

Thrilling, urgent, gut-wrenching, full of suspense;
all so very real in its depiction
of the horrific possibilities
lurking in the margins
of the mundane.
He leads us through a highly complex plot
whose disparate elements
he holds in perfect balance
- until that final, startling revelation

(When asked to review a manuscript in 50 words or less I had fun with a few different slants on it)

Palladian Books, Bath

NOT ACCORDING TO DARWIN

Which spectral cartographer, combining aesthetics,
science and technique determined
that reality, modelled in ways
that communicate special information,
would become life?
What extrasensory, supernatural or
esoteric skills were required?
Was God a spiritual cartographer?
Not according to Darwin.

Cartographers set traits –
physical, such as roads or land masses
or abstract such a toponyms or political boundaries.
Geologists, oceanographers, astrologists
and others, determine what lies beyond
the cartographer's work.
But who can say with any certainty
what lies beyond life on earth?
Does God determine these things?
Not according to Darwin!

The 'ups' and 'downs', joys and sadness we experience in life
hardly epitomises the terrain of a mapped object
on a two dimensional flat medium.
Any map is a distortion of reality
and the only accurate representation of territory
is an identical copy of reality itself.
By promising everlasting life
does God reinforce reality?
Not according to Darwin.

Historically, maps controlled by human interests
as they were in a colonial context,
were always influenced by social relations
and cultural attitudes
and could never be exact
or objective.
Is God's word objective and exact?
Not according to Darwin.

(Gerardus Mercator - the first cartographer to use longitude and latitude for sailors. He aided the pursuits of traders with his map of the world)

TRIBUTE TO MIKE CATT

In virtually all of the movies I have seen
and all the books I have ever read,
no hero seemed to ever grow old,
or die peacefully lying in his or her bed.
As kids we loved our Wild West heroes
firing six guns from a fiery steed;
against all odds, they saved the day
inspired by conviction, courage or creed.
Or the anti-hero with a wanderlust,
so carefree but walking as tall;
as the Bible told us David was to Goliath,
a brave heart who rose to the call.

One sportsman we know who fits this image
according to the biography "*My story*,"
when others retired after the rugby world cup,
he sought out and found further glory.
No sportsman can truly be classed a hero
until he has risen beyond purification;
when he surmounts the very pinnacle
of what's considered normal aspiration.
If his opponents are truly great and worthy
but our hero remains steadfast and true,
then he becomes for us a sporting legend
one of the rugby world's elitist few.

Though inevitably he had to call it a day
still a legend to many he will be;
a real monument of sporting stature
a lighthouse in a pounding sea.
When finally Catty hung up his boots,
and decided he could no longer play
we hoped that he would remain involved,
not just retire and then fade away
Some men they never rise to be heroes
regardless of the sacrifice and pain
but for one World Cup winner who 'Landed on his feet'
our memories of him will never wane.

(To Mike Catt with thanks for the signed copy of his book "Landing on my feet" he sent me)

About Mike:
South African footballer who became known for his versatility; he was able to play fullback, fly-half, inside centre, outside centre, and wing.

School: He attended Grey High School until 1989.
Date of Birth: 17 September 1971
Place of birth: Port Elizabeth, South Africa
His mother: Anne, was English hence his eligibility to play for England
Trivia: He joined Bath in 1992 as understudy to Stuart Barnes and played his first game against Nottingham RFC. He became the oldest player ever, at age 37, to participate in a Guinness Premiership final in 2009
Appearances: Bath 220; London Irish 46, England 75; Lions 1.
Honours: Already a Member of the Order of the British Empire (MBE), he was appointed Officer of the Order of the British Empire (OBE) in the 2011 New Year Honours for services to rugby

PROPHESY

John & Carol, two lovers, rode together in deathly silence
returning home early from a less than memorable date.
John, worried and very confused, sensed that all was not well,
but hoped it was mere tiredness, albeit the hour was not late.

The long, painful silence was broken only for a brief moment
when Carol asked John to please pull over into a lay-by.
She wanted to talk, there was something she had to say,
the signs were not good as first she sobbed, then began to cry.

She told him that her feelings for him had now sadly changed
and, with her voice quivering, each word sticking in her throat.
She told him that she felt it was time they both moved on.
A tear slid down his cheek as he passed her a folded note.

At that moment, a drunk driver came speeding towards them
travelling too fast down a street where the lighting was poor.
He swerved completely out of control, braked far too late
and with a sickening crunch, smashed into the driver's side door.

John had no chance and died instantly as did the drunk driver.
Carol survived and was dragged from the car by a passer-by.
In the ambulance she remembered the note John had given her,
tearfully she read it. "Without your love, I will surely die."

AT ONE WITH NATURE

Something is bothering me about our world today,
it is what this generation calls the modern way.
Talking, reading or occasionally we would type,
now they just read screens, go to Facebook or Skype.

The age of liberation is now become one of obsession,
a smart phone today man's most cherished possession.
No longer are they gregarious but are happy being alone,
blogging, tweeting and texting from their i-Phone.

When people become numbers and reading a tweet,
no desire to telephone or to go meet and greet.
Kidding themselves into believing they're connecting,
when all they are really doing is tweeting or texting.

It requires no imagination, just a vacuous mind,
no need to be creative, just a new App to find.
They have all made i-Phone covers for their hearts,
but never learned the basics of where love starts.

Who was it that created these anti-social disasters,
making kids beholden to these hi-tech masters?
In a bygone era time together we would spend,
now they click a button to visit a special friend.

Fingers have travelled many miles on a keyboard,
but overall physical fitness now strikes a sour chord.
Whatever happened to having fun with your mates,
are they too worshipping at the temple of Bill Gates?

Yours truly is an aging island in a bygone era sea,
navigating best I can this ocean of technology.
But I smile when the environment young folk bemoan,
typing "I am one with nature" into their i-Phone.

SOUL AWAKENED

What is the muse to her own sorrow
and the digger of her grave,
the painter of her ocean view
and every fatal wave?

What is the shadow of her Father,
mysteriously lacking light,
the sky devoid of any stars
a ghostly pale moonlight?

What makes music with no words;
makes love without reason,
a dreamer with submission
a trial for every season?

What torments with cold intentions,
her nemesis scared and shaken,
bold and pure - the lost and found,
it's her inmost soul awakened

MAIDEN OR MOUNTAIN

Tall, statuesque; her magnificence undeniable,
that breath-taking, picture postcard beauty
prepotent as she towers above me.
Regal and supreme, she emanates majesty
with an exquisite, graceful demeanour
that beckons me with unspoken words.
Her allure is both enduring and enticing,
mesmerising all who look in her direction.

One can't help but admire the contours
of soft rolling mounds and gentle valleys.
Beneath clouds blanketed with passion
naked limbs hunger for the touch of rain.
Green plains in sexy flower dresses
belly dance to the whispering breeze.
Expectations of undiscovered treasures
fire my fanciful and fertile imagination.

The sun rises slowly above the horizon
casting a shadow across her face.
Beneath a cloud-like veil I glimpse
provocative eyes shrouded in mystery.
Challenging, beckoning with enticement.
I am bound up in a mystical turmoil
that dominates and, like morphinism
I hesitate, intimidated and confused.

The desire to explore virgin territory
is irresistible and seductively erotic.
Foreplay of reconnaissance, caution and fear
a prelude to taking the first, tentative steps.
The stimulatingly evanescent caresses
wreak havoc with my senses.
Highly charged currents that flow
unrestricted around her coveted reactive spaces.

In a post-coital state I lie back dreaming,
reflecting upon my fulfilling achievement.
Alone, with thoughts in time displaced,
I wonder, does she spellbind others this way
or in my silent muse am I the only one
transformed and floored by her beauty?
The climax achieved, the summit reached
exhilarating, energy sapping and emotional.

But then who cares; I came and I conquered.
Touching some quintessential passion,
that promised untold pleasures
the exalted summit was scaled.
The memory of her naked splendour
never grows old and her beauty still remains
indelibly imprinted on my erotic mind.
The experience a paradigm for young lovers

OLD VALUES

Values; the inescapable measure of man's soul
precious, immortal, commanding.
Underrated in the league of human virtues
they are no more in demand,
The tide is turning!
The wind is blowing from a different direction
and the climate we knew rapidly changing.
Old values are being smashed on the rocks
by the powerful tides of tomorrow's world.
Time certainly does not stand still.
Occasionally it repeats itself
in an epitaph to yesterday,
a legacy of the past.
Values that were, are lost in memory,
Ignorant of past values, the tide turns.

In the undertow of cold or torrid waves,
spent dreams now abide,
and the rigours of age and ages take their toll.
Memory is a fickle lover, like waves
succumbing to the tide
with dreams and values blown off with the wind.
Those scraps of treasured memories,
ideals linked to bygone dreams.
Important somethings, maybe everythings,
unrealised and compartmentalised.
Ignorant of past values, the tide turns.

Seismic social changes aggravate the censorious
and the weight of the past prays
burdening the living.
Chronicling the history of countless generations
we can only scratch our heads
and feel a sense of awe.
The path one takes, or the waves one creates
no one will face or walk for you
Relentlessly the tide rushes in and rushes out
leaving in its wake shifting sands.
Ignorant of past values, the tide turn.

OUTCOMES

Marching onwards regardless of past glories
staring ahead, oblivious to past virtues or values.
Eyes wide open, but unable to comprehend,
none so blind as those
who have no wish to see.

One day they will be awakened by hindsight
and will again praise those values
personified by our ancestors.
We will belatedly come to realise
that in sole pursuit of self
we nurture fallibility.

Today's generation fostered with failure
discarded values their kismet.
The hard, cruel face of 'freedom'
beckoning people to martyrdom,
killed by the people, for the people.
Driven forward by empty lies,
fuelling flames of selfishness and greed,
individuality forsaken, minds imploding.

Hypocritical creed gave in to self aggrandisement,
never really making progress or peace
only descending into insanity,
giving in to avarice.
Our leaders now luminaries of loathing,
with their pathetic, pandering paradoxes,
no longer leading with their lies
but now resting in rebellious retribution.

Within nations no longer bounded by norms
or welded together by camaraderie,
the once proud individual soul becomes
isolated, alone and exposed.
Belatedly we recognised the value of 'values'
that which once gave us our own originality.
The annals will have turned full circle
and history will finally repeat itself.

NEW VALUES

Gingerly, as we pick our way around tidal pools
it dawns on us that all the joy we anticipated
may still be out there - in the future.
There may still be a wondrous revival
if we can but keep our eyes on the prize.
Only those with vision and foresight
will be able to discern
what constitutes the hereafter
as opposed to the 'gone before'.
Blind to hindsight
eyes open to opportunity,
history has yet to be made.

Looking around us we see the coming generation
working diligently to fulfil their aspirations.
What will become of these youths
in the next few years?
Some may die fighting on foreign shores,
others will die young due to bad habits.
Some may achieve great success
others may die trying
others will just die.
Few will mourn the passing of a bygone era.
Ignorant of past values and traditions,
history is unlikely to repeat itself.

The years come and go so quickly
technology bringing with it such immediacy.
Almost compressing the future
into the present.
Letting us gaze optimistically
through the windmills of our minds
to the unscripted, untrodden
but wildly exciting future.
Ignoring the fundamental enjoyment
of historical values - wisdom, truth,
goodness, justice and love,
they cannot be resurrected
From the vortex known as the past.

comes a breath of fresh air.
What we once dreamed actually remains alive;
we will not be daunted by voices of despair.
or held back by past protocols.
Self replaces team, success at all cost;
divided we celebrate individuality.
Nothing in heaven or upon earth
shall determine our global fate.
Time and tide stands still for no man
and just as history does not always repeat itself
past values will, sadly, never return.

WASTELAND OF A SOUL

Lazily my mind wavers as I lay in the shadows
staring out of the soulless bedroom window
seeing the sun sink and dark clouds assemble.
Tiny golden flecks imprinting on the soft white
laces and trims, signal evening's arrival.
Creating shadows and eerie images
as the last rays of brilliance
turn into a sun-kissed glowing ember
of a sad and forlorn goodbye.
Then, ever so softly fading
into dullness and cloudless cold.

Like a precursor to yet another deflated dream
the colours change and gloom descends.
My head spins as inner thoughts become restless
and the noise of uncertainty is rearranged.
The mind rallies but the heart groans in
yet another self-inflicted damning of emotions.
Tormenting what is left of self-respect
hating myself, afraid and desperately lonely,
I lie still with a sad, hardened heart.
In the sobering evening shadows
I am disarmed and defenceless.

The night falls and darkness engulfs my space;
fear grips me and mysterious shadows dance
to the wonderful moonlit music of silence.
I listen, searching still for what is left.
No longer any traces of the daytime sun
whose magnificence and radiance
had once touched the leaves of laughter.
Slowly, my will to live starts to desert me;
feelings numbed until they actually die.
Half buried amidst all the other corpses
that make up the wasteland of my soul.

TWENTY FOUR HOURS IN SUMMER

Clouds like black silk shrouds obscure all but a part of the retiring
moonlight.
Silence claims the early morning skies as nature slumbers.
Slowly, the orange upper limb of the sun comes up over the horizon
chased only by a few wispy clouds that streak the pale blue sky.
A chill rustles through the leaves creating background music
- the harmonious voice of creation.
From the initial gentle, subtle wing music of bees and flies
to the crescendo of an awakening dawn chorus.
Dew sprinkled across the landscape begins to sparkle
like a sea of jewels or perhaps morning tears
glistening on the cool grass.

Slowly the sun rises up from the horizon like a golden balloon;
an iridescent light of golden splendour.
The last few remaining clouds slowly vacate the pale blue sky.
There is just enough breeze to stir the bustling, restless leaves
and, like a Mexican wave, sets in motion an endless ocean of corn.
The air is alive and compliments the sweet aroma that weaves within.
Acorns and horse chestnut husks nest in secret whorls of grass
beneath luxuriant trees swaying majestically in the now clear blue sky.
A waterfall that falls leisurely from the stream on a plateau above
feeds a natural, languid rock pool and
creates a rainbow in the spray that sprinkles environed plants.
The gentle breeze turns luke-warm but carries still the unmistakable
aroma of wheat and wild flowers.
The scent neither disperses or dissolves in the midday dew
or floats away into the afternoon clouds
but lingers on throughout the remainder of the day.

All too soon the smells, sounds and colours of the day start to retreat
Awe grows on the way to the summer twilight
as early the waning light fades and Harbingers the coming of night.
The sun sets with pale fluttering and greenness dims in each grass
blade;
there begins a pleading plaintiveness in the wind's caress.
Myriads of lingering stars align and moonlight shines,
reflecting off the placid pool

Lithe swallows muster and dive before retiring for the night.
A silvery, hauntingly ghostly mist wanders through the rushes
moved by each passing breeze.
The horizon lights up in swirls of orange and pink,
fading to blue then purple.
Black silk clouds again shrouds the retiring moon in darkness.
and Nature sleeps (all except the nocturnal beetles).

DEPRESSION ALLIANCE

Like deathly silence on the battlefield
a sense of foreboding drifts over me,
cutting the barbwire of dysphoria
that tightly wraps my mind's eye.
I will let the dreaded demons soar,
floating 'midst shooting stars and rainbows,
to a place where there is still hope,
a place where peace is a reality.

Storms pass and I raise the sails of hope
but there's very little wind to fill them;
floundering like a helpless, rudderless ship
I float in the dark deep ocean of nothing.
The horizon I seek has long disappeared,
lost beneath a cloudy, grey leaden sky;
as I cast my doubts into the wind
I try not to let the demons see me cry.

It is a cold, dark tormented world I frequent,
full of uncertainty, questions and confusion;
but wait; within the darkness of shadows
there is a faint, miniscule shard of light.
I claw my way forward with every cell of me,
fighting fear and with an aching soul;
I reach for it, long for it, pray for it
my last remaining tie to a fading world

They call it *Depression Alliance*
that tiny shard of light that is hope.

WHY THE CHARITY DEPRESSION ALLIANCE?

Before my son Jason died aged just 32, we tried desperately for three years to find help. The NHS seemed totally ill equipped to deal with any mental health issues and the only solution seemingly open to us was to pay £25,000 for him to be given ECT treatment at The Priory. Sadly he died the night before this treatment was due to begin.

Since losing Jason, I felt compelled to try and help others whose lives have been touched by depression. It was during that search that I met Emer O'Neill, the CEO of Depression Alliance.

Emer invited me to join the DA board at a time when they were buildingthe foundations of "Friends in Need," a new service that would significantly increase their ability to make contact with the many thousands of people who we know are struggling with the loneliness and isolation that comes with depression. What drew me most to Depression Alliance was the fact it is the leading national charity specifically for people with depression in England. It is a membership organisation and for the past 35 years has been coordinating self-help groups and other support services across the country. Their mission is simply put: "We bring people together to make them happier".

In November 2013 I was invited to 10 Downing Street to help celebrate the soon to be publicly launched 'Friends in Need' campaign. This programme combines not only the core services that DA has run for years, but new ways to engage people affected by depression; people like my family, who walk that heart-wrenching journey beside a loved one with the condition.

Depression Alliance's services are not medical, but work alongside health services by providing support and understanding to those who are affected by depression.

I chose DA because of the simplicity of their aims and I know from firsthand experience that there is a real need for their work.

The proceeds of this book are all going to help DA reach everyone facing depression across the country; people of all ages, cultures and walks of life through the Friends in Need in community, and by so doing, provide people with that life line which is so essential to recovery from depression.

The following are just some of the many ways DA can help:
1. Local Support
The national network of self-help groups enable people affected by depression to share experiences and coping strategies with others in similar situations

2. Publications

DA has a range of leaflets, publications and posters that offer in depth information

3. Making your voice heard

DA works with healthcare professionals to secure better service provision for people affected by depression and lobbies government to influence policy-making in this mental health field.

4. Raising awareness

Influenced by the experiences of people with depression, DA raises awareness of the realities of the illness amongst the general public with a variety of influential campaigns throughout the year.

5. Supporter Scheme

By becoming a supporter of Depression Alliance you receive the quarterly newsletter Single Step, have exclusive access to our supporter services as well as complimentary literature.

6. Research

Depression Alliance works in partnership with universities, health professionals and other voluntary organisations to research the causes, treatments and instances of depression in the UK. DA uses the findings of its research to educate and inform health professionals, government, and the general public via the media.

Having been so impressed by all the work they do, I joined the Appeal Board and am dedicating the proceeds of this book to DA.

The Friends in Need initiative:

Those running DA know from what their members have told them over the years, that it is the loneliness and isolation which depression brings that makes recovery so much harder to maintain. They know that there are people coming to use their services who haven't found enough support, or the right type of support, and that's why DA are delighted to be able to change that.

The Friends in Need website was officially launched in January 2014 and provides an opportunity for people to chat online, meet up in groups, take part in activities and attend events in close proximity to where they live or work.

DA hopes that for many people who are looking for support that this will be their first port of call.

Visit the website and watch the video to find out more about DA
http://www.depressionalliance.org

In summary:

- Friends in Need will end the loneliness that comes with depression.
- It is an on-line and off-line community, linking people together for social support – events, activities and meet-ups to maintain wellbeing and recovery. It is for anyone affected by depression.
- Friends in Need is based on the Five Ways to Wellbeing research and informed by DA's 30 years of bringing people together to make them happier.
- Friends in Need will grow through a national network of volunteer champions.
- DA is working with partners who will help them deliver Friends in Need to their sector or area e.g. Charity for Civil Servants, Specific project for ending loneliness and isolation for older people in Windsor and Maidenhead. By working with partners DA will have much more impact.

Depression Alliance is the leading UK charity for people affected by depression.

Registered UK charity No. 1096741.
Registered Company No 4253700

Depression Alliance,
20 Great Dover Street,
London SE1 4LX.
Tel: 020 7407 7584.

DepressionAlliance
www.depressionalliance.org

ABOUT THE ARTIST: Loui Jover

Loui was **born** in Debeljaca, a small town in former Yugoslavia. He was still a baby when his parents migrated to Australia after a short spell in Austria. His freelance art career truly began after a spell in the army and then a brief period as joint owner of a small graphic art business. Loui reflects on the influences that lead him to become the accomplished artist he is today. "I saw Picasso's works in Paris, Vincent's in Britain, Klee in Berlin. I saw the Mona Lisa and Rodin's Atelier. Undoubtedly all these influenced my development, but in the end  it's always the more intimate moments that affect one's sensibilities. I loved the narrow run down areas of Paris streets more then the grand processions, I liked the damp crowded spaces of London better then Trafalgar Square. I liked the wild and undisciplined feel of Montenegro or the ancient walls of Dubrovnik, the brooding city of Belgrade with its bombed out buildings and the crazy back streets of Rome. All this has been invaluable to the formation of my artistic ideals". Loui very kindly allowed me to reproduce many of his pictures in this book to help raise money for the charity.
See more of Loui's work on *http://louijover.tumblr.com*

PHOTOGAPHER: Peter Sherrard has been a professional photographer for over twenty years. Specialising in book jacket and stock photography, he has provided the images for hundreds of book covers, in many different genres.
For over ten years he has been working for one of the largest and most successful picture libraries in the world.
Pete was kind enough to contribute to this charitable endeavour by donating his time and expertise to produce the front cover. See more of Pete's work on the website *http://petesherrard.com*

ABOUT THE AUTHOR

"Poetry often enters through the window of irrelevance"
so, please keep all your windows open!

 All the poems featured in Stan Frith's second book of verse *Behind the Smile,* again house the author's feelings and experiences in his more recent journey through life as well as the things he saw and felt along the way. Like most poets, he continues to enjoy a strong sense of the evanescence of experience.

A lifelong admirer of poets who he feels 'run in the bloodstream' or are 'evocative for a lifetime' – Blake, Browning, Burns, Byron, Keats, Kipling, Longfellow, Milton, Shakespeare, Shelley, Tennyson, Thomas etc his work tends to follow a traditionalist vein. However, in this book he has featured a variety of writing forms and structures.

The author spent his formative years in Kent, and two thirds of his working life travelling the globe with Texas Instruments. The final third of his career he spent in retail and then an entrepreneur before the rigours of boardroom life finally gave way to his lifelong passion – writing. Over the years his stories, articles and poems have featured in numerous publications. As with *Time In Between,* several of the poems featured in this book have won critical acclaim, awards and prizes.

Stan Frith is Chairman of Fidelius Financial Holdings Ltd and of Bath Golf Club. His other interests include a great love of rugby and golf, as well as devoting time to the charity Depression Alliance, with which he has enjoyed an association since the tragic death of his son Jason.

He is married to wife Angela, has two sons – Rory and Jamie and currently lives in Bath, England.

As can be seen from the Acknowledgements at the front of the book, his wish is that all proceeds from the sale of *Behind the Smile* go to the charity Depression Alliance in the sincere hope this endeavour will invoke in others newfound hope, inspiration and stability. You can visit Stan's website at *www.stanfrith.co.uk* and also his charity of choice website *www.depressionalliance.org* for more information.